Pages 8/9:
Moorish riches in
Seville's golden age

INSIGHT POCKET GUIDE

Seville
CORDOBA & GRANADA

APA PUBLICATIONS
Part of the Langenscheidt Publishing Group

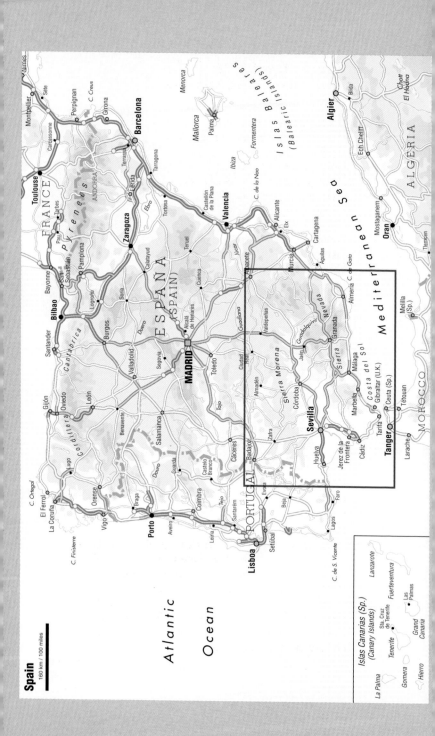

Welcome!

This guidebook combines the interests and enthusiasms of two of the world's best-known information providers: Insight Guides, who have set the standard for visual travel guides since 1970, and Discovery Channel, the world's premier source of non-fiction television programming.

Its aim is to help visitors get the most out of a short stay out of Southern Spain's three great cities, Seville, Córdoba and Granada. Spain has changed over the past few decades, and nowhere faster than in Andalusia where huge infrastructural investments were made for the universal jamboree of Expo '92 in Seville. The area will always be a hotbed of Spanish cliché – the birthplace of flamenco, the cradle of bullfighting, a playground for gypsy passion – but it is now also a fashionable, hi-tech capital of southern Europe.

Insight Guides' specialist on the region, Nigel Tisdall, has designed a series of itineraries to help visitors get the most out of the cities during a short stay. Seville's Cathedral and Giralda tower, Córdoba's Mezquita and Granada's Alhambra are all explored in detail, but the guide also takes one into the old Jewish and Moorish quarters beyond the blockbuster sights, with frequent recommendations for shopping, lunch and tapas en route. Supporting the itineraries are sections on history and culture, eating out, shopping and practical information, including a list of recommended hotels.

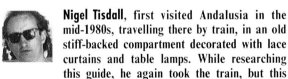

Nigel Tisdall, first visited Andalusia in the mid-1980s, travelling there by train, in an old stiff-backed compartment decorated with lace curtains and table lamps. While researching this guide, he again took the train, but this time a Talgo, a sleek express complete with video screens. He describes Andalusia as one of the most exhilarating regions of Spain.

C O N T E N T S

Pages 2/3:
Seville's Plaza
de España

Itálica

Roman and Moorish Andalusia

The Río Guadalquivir is one of Spain's great rivers. Rising in the mountains of north-eastern Jaén, its waters wind west for some 375 miles (603.5km), carving an ever-widening valley that culminates in Las Marismas, the broad marshlands that stall its entry into the Atlantic beside the sherry town of Sanlúcar de Barrameda. Now bloated with silt, it is but a portly descendant of the fast-flowing, frequently-flooding Baetis (Blessed) that the Romans knew. When their fleets arrived here in the 1st century BC they could sail upriver as far as Córdoba, a strategic point already colonised by Phoenician, Carthaginian and Iberian settlers.

The Romans laid the ground plan of southern Spain, building roads, bridges and aqueducts and establishing Córdoba, the home of Seneca and Lucan, as the capital of Hispania Ulterior. They redeveloped many of the pre-historic settlements bordering the Baetis, including Hispalis (now Seville), Carmona and Itálica. Rich archaeological finds have since been made in this vicinity, many of which now grace the museums and stately homes of Seville and Córdoba. Most famous of all is the Carambolo treasure in Seville's Museo Arqueológico, gold jewellery that testifies to the wealth of the kingdom of Tartessus that flourished here in the 8th and 9th centuries BC. Near Santiponce (now on the western outskirts of Seville) you can wander amidst the crumbling ruins of Roman Itálica, birthplace of the emperors Trajan and Hadrian, while at Carmona a necropolis and amphitheatre survive.

With the fall of the Roman Empire, Spain came under the influence of the Visigoths who set up their capital in Toledo – some of their fountains, arches and columns can still be seen lurking inside An-

Culture

dalusian monuments constructed many centuries later. In AD 711 the Moors – principally Arabs and North African Berbers – landed at Tarifa. Their advance was phenomenal: within seven years they had conquered virtually all of the peninsula. What had begun as a daring foray was to result in eight centuries of Moorish rule and the flowering of one of Europe's greatest civilisations.

The Moors called their new land 'al-Andalus', and the river that fed it 'Guad-al-Quivir', the Great River. Córdoba was its capital – by the 10th century it had become the most important city in Europe, four times its present size, with a university, libraries, public baths, workshops, street-lighting and over a thousand mosques. The greatest of these, La Mezquita, still stands as a testimony to this golden age which reached its apogee with the construction of the palaces at Medinat al-Zahra (now Medina Azahara on the outskirts of Córdoba). Today their partly restored ruins barely hint at the opulence of this royal pleasure park which had its own zoo, mint, fabric factory and arsenal. At its centre stood a pool filled with mercury that when stirred sent the sunlight flashing round the surrounding marble patios, roofed with gold and silver tiles.

Fabulous wealth grew from the Moors' talent for irrigation in the rich lands of the Guadalquivir valley. The Greeks had introduced the vine and the olive – both cultivated intensively by the Romans – but it was the Arabs who added the orange and the almond tree, along with rice, aubergines, saffron, cotton, silk-farming, Merino sheep and herbs, spices and fruits. They also, like the Phoenicians before them and the British long after, exploited the mineral resources of the surrounding sierras.

Medina Azahara

Moorish splendour

The Reconquest

Inevitably, it did not last. By the 11th century the refined glory of the Umayyad Caliphate had disintegrated into feuding *taifas* (factional kingdoms), easily overrun by the puritanical Almoravids whose Berber armies were summoned to prevent a Christian reconquest. They were in turn succeeded by the broader-minded Almohads who established their capital in Seville – the greatest of the *taifas* – and bequeathed us the Giralda and Torre del Oro as souvenirs of their reign.

In 1212 the Christians defeated the Almohads at Las Navas de Tolosa in the Sierra Morena, a turning point in the 700-year *Reconquista*. By 1236 Ferdinand III had captured Córdoba and 12 years later Seville fell. His success was aided by the complicity of the first Nasrid king, Ibn-al-Ahmar, who had retreated from Jaén to establish a power base in the mountains of the Sierra Nevada by taking over the former Almoravid capital of Granada.

By signing a peace treaty with the Christians, the kingdom of Granada – which roughly covered the modern provinces of Málaga, Granada and Almería – survived as a vassal state for the next 250 years. The city flourished as refugees and artisans from other captured cities arrived, enabling the introvert Nasrid kings to build what has become a poignant memorial to the swan-song days of al-Andalus, the Alhambra. At the same time a Christian king, Pedro the Cruel, was also employing Moorish craftsmen to build another tribute to this fading world – the Alcázar in Seville.

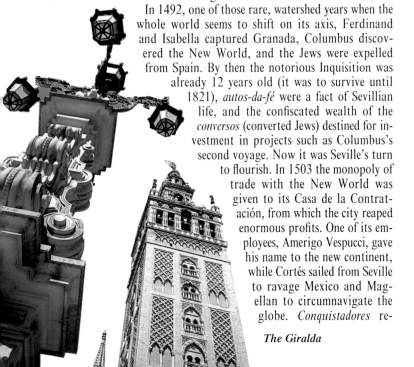

In 1492, one of those rare, watershed years when the whole world seems to shift on its axis, Ferdinand and Isabella captured Granada, Columbus discovered the New World, and the Jews were expelled from Spain. By then the notorious Inquisition was already 12 years old (it was to survive until 1821), *autos-da-fé* were a fact of Sevillian life, and the confiscated wealth of the *conversos* (converted Jews) destined for investment in projects such as Columbus's second voyage. Now it was Seville's turn to flourish. In 1503 the monopoly of trade with the New World was given to its Casa de la Contratación, from which the city reaped enormous profits. One of its employees, Amerigo Vespucci, gave his name to the new continent, while Cortés sailed from Seville to ravage Mexico and Magellan to circumnavigate the globe. *Conquistadores* re-

The Giralda

turned laden with gold and new found curiosities such as peppers, tomatoes, quinine and tobacco.

By 1588 Seville had a population of at least 80,000 and a stature equal to that of Venice. From here it embarked on a slow, glorious descent into decadence, a decline exacerbated by the expulsion of the *moriscos* (converted Moors) in 1610 and a great plague in 1649. During the 16th and 17th centuries Seville acted as a cosmopolitan transit point for trade, administration and emigration – its Lonja (Exchange), paid for by a quarter per cent tax on the import of silver, is now the Archive of the Indies where the signatures of these early colonisers are recorded.

These were heady, gold rush days of wealth and decay for the city. Cervantes (1547–1616), who served time in Seville's prison, recorded its colourful, roguish underworld in his novels, while Murillo (1617–82) painted the beggared characters of its crowded streets. The Church, its coffers filled to bursting by the activities of the Inquisition, acquired a wealth that enabled it to build itself luxury city-centre sanctuaries that still force pedestrians to make boring circumnavigatory detours. At one point the city had over 70 convents, a glut only excused by the fact that they were often decorated by paintings and sculpture executed by artists such as Velázquez, Cano, Zurbarán, Murillo and Leal – all members of what is referred to now as the Seville School. Their works can be seen in

Bust of Cano, one of the Seville School of artists

Seville's excellent Fine Arts museum.

In 1717 Seville received official recognition of its decline when the silting of the Guadalquivir forced the Casa de la Contratación to be moved south to Cádiz. Córdoba and Granada were now provincial backwaters in a demoralised Spain whose empire had been shrivelled by the War of the Spanish Succession (1701–14). In the course of the 18th and 19th centuries Andalusia became a romantic fiction to enchant Northern European audiences – the home of gypsies, brigands, *majos* (dandies) and matadors. Seville was a city of aristocratic seducers called Don Juan and street-wise barbers called Figaro, while a gypsy girl by the name of Carmen worked in the sultry heat of its famous Tobacco Factory.

In reality, however, Andalusia was a place of political chaos and deep poverty; by the beginning of the 19th century 72 percent of the farming land in Seville was owned by an elite and invariably absentee landlord class that comprised barely five percent of its population.

Travellers and Romantics

Poverty contributed to the appeal of southern Spain for the many aristocratic travellers who hired mules, boats and carriages to tour its provinces. They enjoyed its dilapidated state, exotic landscape and Moorish-Oriental heritage. The Alhambra – now a picturesque ruin where picaresque residents caught swallows with fishing rods – inspired much of this Romantic bliss. Washington Irving swam in its ancient pools, Théophile Gautier cooled sherry in its fountains and hotels appeared on the hill beside.

However, it was the comparatively passionate and openly sensual lifestyles of the Andalusians that really set northern hearts pumping. Hans Christian Andersen, visiting Andalusia in the 1860s, openly admitted his disappointment that he had not had 'just a little encounter with bandits'. One intrepid lady traveller, journeying down to the Sahara at a similar time, confessed that after hearing a guitarist play in Granada 'you are ready to make love and war'.

Spain – which principally meant Andalusia to these visitors – was in, a fashion encouraged by the victories of the Peninsular War (1809–14), its cheapness and the growth of trade interests such as sherry and mining. Granada and Seville topped the bill of places to see: 'Seville, the marvel of Andalusia, can be seen in a week' declared Richard Ford in his 1845 *Handbook for Spain*, a masterly work that did much to put Spain on the tourist map. Córdoba tended to receive, as it does even today, a more perfunctory inspection.

By the end of the 19th century, Spain had lost virtually all of its remaining colonies and still lacked political stability. The nation remained neutral during World War I but in the 1920s became embroiled in a war of independence with its one-time masters, the Berber tribes of Morocco. In an attempt to create a lasting order out of chaos, General Miguel Primo de Rivera as-

Carmen in stone

Columbus Was Everywhere

In 1485 Christopher Columbus (1451–1506) arrived in Spain to seek support for his 'Enterprise of the Indies' – a voyage that would try to reach the fabled shores of the East by sailing west across the Atlantic. Then aged 34, this Genoa-born mariner (who may have been of Spanish-Jewish descent) had prematurely white hair, was a widower with a five-year-old son, and had already sailed as far as Madeira, Iceland and the Gold Coast.

Columbus had just had his project turned down by the Portuguese court. He travelled to Córdoba in 1486 for an audience with Ferdinand and Isabella. The monarchs ordered a commission to assess his proposals which took four years to reach its verdict: 'vain and worthy of all rejection'. Columbus retreated to the monastery of La Rábida, near Huelva, but its prior, who had once been Isabella's confessor, succeeded in getting him recalled to the court.

His demands met, Columbus sailed on 3 August from Palos de la Frontera (near Huelva) with three caravels, *Nina*, *Pinta* and *Santa María*. On 12 October 1492 they sighted land – one of the Bahama Islands – and a few hours later the Spanish flag was planted in the New World.

Columbus made three more voyages. In 1493 he sailed from Cádiz and discovered Puerto Rico and Jamaica; in 1498 he sailed from Sanlúcar de Barrameda and reached the mouth of the Orinoco; finally in 1502 he sailed from Seville and discovered Panama.

In the last decade of his life he made frequent use of a Carthusian monastery to the west of Seville, Santa María de las Cuevas. Here he wrote four autobiographical books, mourned the loss of his governorship over the lands he discovered, and hatched new plans – such as the liberation of Jerusalem. The monastery was completely restored to become the centrepoint of Expo '92 and is now a museum and exhibition space well worth visiting.

Columbus died in Valladolid in 1506, after which the great discoverer's remains went on a mysterious voyage of their own. In 1509 they were brought back to La Cartuja, but were exhumed again in 1536 – perhaps being transferred to Seville's cathedral. Around 1544 they were shipped to the Caribbean island of Santo Domingo (now the Dominican Republic), but were later moved to Havana cathedral; then, in 1899, they were returned to Seville cathedral. What ended up where is anybody's guess, but one thing is certain: an awful lot of places can stand up and say with all honesty 'Columbus was here'.

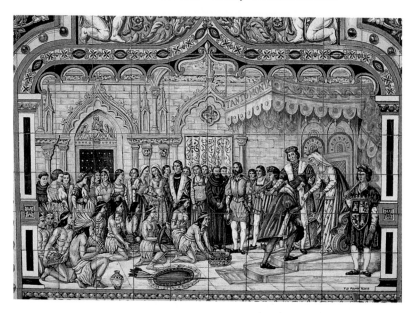

Architectural Terms

Alcázar: Moorish palace

Alcazaba: Moorish castle

Aljibe: cistern

Artesonado: inlaid, coffered wooden ceiling, often with star-shaped patterns

Azulejo: coloured and patterned glazed ceramic tile

Mudéjar: work carried out by Moorish craftsmen under Christian rule

Mozarabic: work carried out by Christian craftsmen under Moorish rule

Patio: inner courtyard

Plateresque: Renaissance style with richly ornamented surface decoration, similar to that wrought by a *platero* (silversmith).

sumed power in a semi-dictatorship which had the concurrence of King Alfonso XIII: the pastiche pavilions built for the 1929 Ibero-American Exposition in Seville are a legacy of his period of power.

In the 1930s Ernest Hemingway wrote his paean to the noble art of bullfighting, *Death in the Afternoon*, and many artists and intellectuals volunteered their support for the Republican cause during the Spanish Civil War (1936–9). Seville, Córdoba and Granada were among the first cities to be taken by Franco's Nationalist forces at the start of this war. Up to a million people lost their lives, including many executed in these cities in the first days. One of them was the Granada-born poet and dramatist, Federico García Lorca.

In the aftermath of World War II, during which Spain remained neutral, the country was left isolated and impoverished. Franco's dictatorship lasted until his death in 1975, a period of steady economic advance scarred by political and cultural repression. Many Andalusians migrated to the northern industrial cities or abroad, leaving the countryside deserted. Franco's acceptance in 1953 of American military bases in exchange for loans, along with Spain's subsequent admission to the UN, accelerated its economic recovery and led to the development of mass tourism during the 1960s.

In 1975, monarchy returned in the shape of King Juan Carlos, soon to be followed by democratic elections. In 1982 the Socialist PSOE party, led by charismatic Sevillian lawyer Felipe González, won a sweeping victory that paved the way for long overdue investment in the region. The great manifestation of this was Expo '92 in Seville, which brought new roads, high-speed trains and a building boom to the regional capital.

And yet, for all the multi-million-peseta *proyectos* and hi-tech facelifts scribbled on the countryside the romantic, rose-in-the-teeth view of Andalusia persists. Not just in the tourist brochures and souvenir stalls but fostered by the Andalusians themselves in their patios, bars, *peñas* (clubs) and *ferias* (fairs). In the countryside, donkeys still plough the fields. Andalusia will always be Spain spiced with the tang of North Africa, a mountain-locked land racked by summer heat and fed by the waters of the Guadalquivir.

Artesonado ceiling work

Historical Outline

c.10,000BC Cave paintings at La Pileta (near Ronda) show there were prehistoric settlers in Andalusia during Palaeolithic times.

2,000–500BC The kingdom of Tartessus flourishes in the area around Seville.

1100BC The Phoenicians found Gadir (Cádiz).

3rd century BC Carthaginian forces conquer Andalusia.

218BC Roman colonisation of Spain begins with the Second Punic War.

1st century BC–3rd century AD The Romans transform Andalusia, developing its agriculture and constructing roads and aqueducts. Itálica, Carmona and Seville are founded; Córdoba becomes the capital of Hispania Ulterior.

400–500AD Spain is dominated by the Visigoths.

711 Moorish armies cross the Straits of Gibraltar, conquering the peninsula within seven years.

756–1031 Umayyad dynasty rules over al-Andalus. Córdoba emerges as the capital of Muslim Spain; work starts on La Mezquita. In 929, Abd ar-Rahman III proclaims caliphate of Córdoba.

1086 The Almoravids, fundamentalist Muslim Berbers, invade Spain. They are expelled in 1147 by the Almohads who build the Great Mosque of Seville, crowned by a minaret, La Giralda.

1212 The Almohads are defeated at the Battle of Las Navas de Tolosa. By 1248, Ferdinand III has taken both Córdoba and Seville.

1237–1492 Nasrid dynasty rules the Kingdom of Granada. Construction of the Alhambra. In the 1360s Pedro the Cruel builds Seville's Alcázar; work starts on the cathedral in 1401.

1469 Marriage of Ferdinand V to Isabella I unites the kingdoms of Aragón and Castile.

1492 Fall of Granada; Columbus discovers America.

1500s Seville is granted a trade monopoly with the New World. Various projects are initiated as a result of the prosperity that follows. During the 1520s work begins on the cathedral in Córdoba's Mezquita, on Granada's cathedral, and on Charles V's palace in the Alhambra.

1600s Prosperity turns to decadence. Seville declines as the Guadalquivir silts up and trade moves to Cádiz. The city produces some of Spain's greatest artists.

1759–88 Charles III introduces enlightened reforms; Seville's Tobacco Factory is completed.

1809–14 Seville, Córdoba and Granada occupied by the French during the Peninsular War.

1800s Spain struggles for political stability and loses its colonies. Romantic travellers discover the region.

1929 Ibero-American Exposition held in Seville.

1936–9 Spanish Civil War: Seville, Córdoba and Granada occupied by Nationalists, parts of eastern Andalusia are held by Republicans.

1975 Franco dies; Juan Carlos I becomes king.

1982 Spain elects a socialist government led by Sevillian Felipe González. Andalusia is granted new autonomous powers.

1986 Spain joins the European Union.

1992 Seville stages Expo '92 and Barcelona hosts the Olympics. 500th anniversary of Columbus's discovery of America.

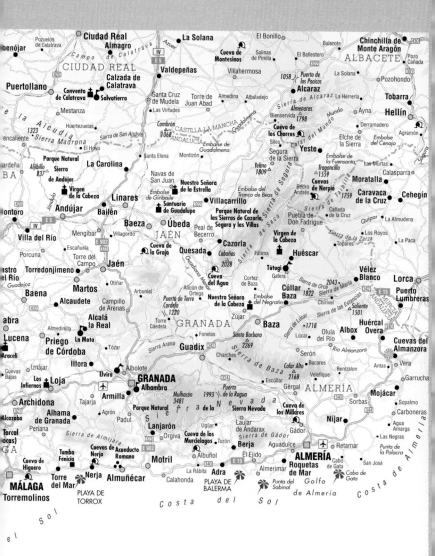
Andalusia

48 km / 30 miles

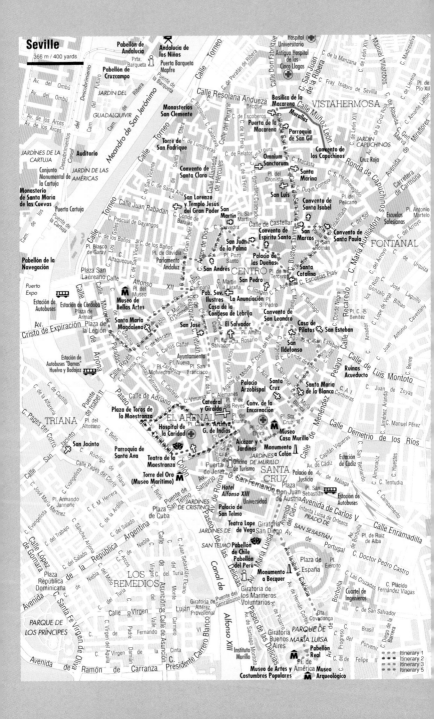

'Let us build a church,' mused the architects of Seville cathedral, 'so big that we shall be held to be insane.' And they did – a vainglorious feat that now squats in the city centre like an obstinate bag-lady. The cathedral, with its great Moorish tower, La Giralda, is Seville's best known landmark, and worth the climb if only to help orientate yourself in what at first seems a hopeless jumble of narrow streets.

Seville has had a long-standing love affair with the grandiose. Next-door to the cathedral you will find Pedro the Cruel's splendid Alcázar, inspired by the Alhambra and later enlarged by Charles V. South of this stands the immense Tobacco Factory, second only to the Escorial in size. Beyond are the expansive remains of the great pavilions, plazas and parks built for the Ibero-American Exposition that almost bankrupted the city in 1929.

You may well judge Seville to be insane (the traffic certainly is) but it has an endearing panache too – most obvious in the city's intense celebration of Semana Santa (Holy Week) and the exuberant Feria (April Fair) that follows it.

Style and energy are part of the Sevillian character, and came to the fore when the city transformed itself into an international stage for Expo '92. The legacy of this investment bonanza is evident everywhere in the city – six new bridges, a spanking new railway station, an expanded airport, a new theatre, restored museums and upgraded hotels.

And yet Seville somehow remains a quiet and intimate city at heart, sensual and faintly decadent, where people live well: sipping their *fino*, washing their *patio* floors, *paseo*-ing four-abreast with triple-decker ice creams. It's such qualities that will make you come back here again and again.

Seville: the cathedral and Giralda

1. Cathedral and Parque de María Luisa

Around the immense cathedral and up the Giralda, its Moorish minaret, for a view of the city. Lunch, and then on foot past where Carmen worked to the venue for Seville's 1929 exhibition, the Parque de María Luisa.

Breakfast in Seville is a brisk, private affair – perhaps a *café con leche* and some *tostada* smeared with olive oil or fish paste, taken standing at the bar in a mood of pensive solemnity. **Bar Los Principes** (Calle Arfe 7) evokes this big city mood admirably, while **Bar Ibense Bornay**, on the junction of Avenida de la Constitución and Calle Almirantazgo, is the ideal place for a quick *café* before you tackle Seville's monster cathedral (open Monday–Saturday 11am–5pm, Sunday 2–4pm).

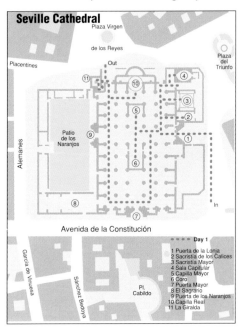

Seville Cathedral

Plaza Virgen de los Reyes

Out

Plaza del Triunfo

Placentines

Alemanes

Patio de los Naranjos

In

Avenida de la Constitución

García de Viñuesa

Sánchez Bedoya

Pl. Cabildo

- - - - **Day 1**

1 Puerta de la Lonja
2 Sacristía de los Cálices
3 Sacristía Mayor
4 Sala Capitular
5 Capilla Mayor
6 Coro
7 Puerta Mayor
8 El Sagrario
9 Puerta de los Naranjos
10 Capilla Real
11 La Giralda

The **Cathedral Santa María de la Sede** began life in 1401 and occupies the former site of a great mosque built by the Almohads in 1172 – its immense size clearly results from the Christian architects' desire to trump the grandeur of their 'heathen' predecessors. Only St Paul's in London and St Peter's in Rome are larger. On first arriving in Seville, you will have passed its rambling exterior, surrounded by enchained Roman pillars taken from Itálica. The adjoining steps, **Las Gradas,** were for many centuries Seville's main meeting-place.

If you're crossing from the Bar Ibense Bornay be sure to look up as you wait (and wait) for the lights to change – above the cathedral you will have a clear view of **La Giralda** and the silhouette of its crowning weather-vane (*giraldillo*), a revolving bronze statue of Faith added in the 16th century (now replaced with a more recent copy).

There are several entrances to the cathedral. On the southern side is the Puerta de Palos door, leading to the **Capilla Real**, the Royal Chapel. This chapel is reserved for those who want to pray, as opposed to tourists, but there is nothing to stop you from peeking in as long as you are not outrageously dressed and you are suitably silent and respectful. The area is fenced off from the rest of the cathedral, and the chapel itself concealed behind a massive curtain. It is dedicated to the Virgen de los Reyes, and a

Detail from the cathedral door

silver urn contains the relics of King Ferdinand III (who expelled the Moors from Seville and Córdoba); nearby lie his wife Beatrice and son Alfonso X (the Wise).

Leave the chapel and walk around the cathedral to the visitors' entrance. The entrance for tour groups is on the eastern side of the cathedral, and for individuals through the **Puerta del Perdón** on the northern side. Both lead into the **Patio de los Naranjos**, a courtyard lined with orange trees, a legacy of the original mosque. It seems inconceivable that this peaceful courtyard, was a notorious sanctuary for criminals in the 16th century.

The **Puerta del Lagarto** (Gate of the Lizard, named for the life-sized wooden alligator hanging incongruously from the ceiling) takes you into the cathedral's interior. Immediately to your left is the entrance to the Giralda, the original Moorish minaret which was capped with a Christian belfry, the ultimate *Reconquista* symbol. Climbing it is like watching a slide show of the city: 34 ramps and a flight of steps later you emerge beneath its awesome bells for a glorious view over Seville. Here you'll find not only a classic Andalusian skyline of white-washed houses and terracotta-tile roofs, for centuries pierced only by the domes and bell-towers of the city's churches and convents, but also the new-money monuments that have recently transformed the city.

To the west, beyond the bullring, are the new bridges built for Expo 92 (including the brilliant wishbone arch of the Puente de la Barqueta); to the east is the futuristic railway station, Santa Justa.

Return down the spiralling ramps of the Giralda. Dominating the scene ahead of you is the *coro* (choir) and **Capilla Mayor** (main chapel), while the depths of the cathedral's cavernous interior stretch to the right.

Take a pew to study the Capilla Mayor's huge *retablo*, a deluge of gold

The Giralda

Ceramic from the city of oranges

that was begun in 1482 by the Flemish sculptor Pieter Dancar and completed 82 years later.

At the opposite side of the high altar from where you entered, inside the Puerta de la Lonja (completed at the start of this century) and usually surrounded by a small crowd of sightseers, you'll spot the oversized tomb of Christopher Columbus, supported by four pallbearers representing the kingdoms of Castile, León, Aragón and Navarre (see 'Columbus Was Everywhere' in *History and Culture*).

Turn right here to explore the depths of the cathedral. Wandering on the outside of the choir, you will realise that the cathedral is virtually a city within a city, terraced with little side chapels, adorned with statues and tombs, full of dusty corners housing long-forgotten memorials. You will come to the **Sagrario**, the Tabernacle Chapel, in effect a church within a church where many Sevillians prefer to attend mass (access from the Avenida de la Constitución). Beyond it at the far end of the cathedral is the huge, rarely-opened **Puerta Mayor**.

Backtrack past the Columbus tomb and towards the cathedral exit to inspect a series of side rooms housing religious treasures. Beyond the chapel of Los Dolores is the **Sacristía de los Cálices**: amongst its works of art you'll encounter a common anachronistic depiction – this one by Goya – of the Giralda and

Bells in the Giralda

two 3rd-century Sevillian martyrs, Santa Justa and Santa Rufina, who escaped death in the lions' den. Next door is the **Sacristía Mayor** with more sacrilegiously-displayed works by Zurbarán, Murillo and van Dyck, along with some of the venerated relics that are paraded through the streets during Semana Santa. In the far corner of the cathedral, next to rooms exhibiting clerical vestments and illuminated manuscripts, a curved passage leads to the Sala Capitular, with an *Immaculate Conception* by Murillo.

After exploring the cathedral you'll be ready for lunch – head for the **Cervecería Giralda** (Calle Mateos Gago 1), straight ahead from the Cathedral exit, across the **Plaza Virgen de los Reyes**. If you arrive before 1.30pm you should be able to get a table in this busy *tapas* bar – look on the blackboard for the *raciones* on offer that day, which normally include typical Sevillian dishes like *huevos a la flamenca* (eggs with ham and vegetables) and *cazuela Tio Pepe* (casserole with sherry). For a more upstage meal consider the **El Giraldillo** restaurant – it is touristy and expensive but the view from its tables is priceless. Whatever you choose, do

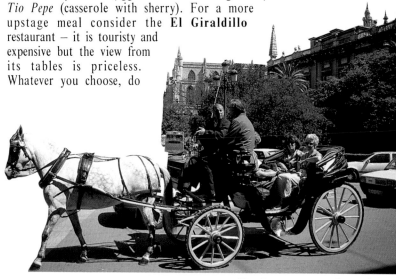

Tourist transport to the park

linger a moment in the Plaza de los Virgen Reyes – even more romantic at night when its monumental lamp-post is lit.

In the afternoon your itinerary leads idly towards the shady bliss of the Parque de María Luisa. You can ride there in style by horse and carriage – there are several *coches de caballos* ranks around the cathedral. Negotiate a price first which will be at least 3,000 pesetas per person depending how far you ride – official prices can be checked at the Tourist Office round the corner at Avenida de la Constitución 21. Otherwise continue back towards the cathedral entrance, turning left into the Plaza del Triunfo where a column celebrates Seville's survival of the 1755 earthquake that devastated Lisbon. Continue back to Avenida de la Constitución and turn left – en route you will pass the back of the Lonja and the entrance to the Reales Alcázares (see Itinerary 2).

Whispering statues in the Parque de María Luisa

Avenida de la Constitución culminates in the Puerta de Jerez and a Grand Prix of traffic. Bear left around this roundabout to reach a luxury oasis, the **Hotel Alfonso XIII.** Opened in 1928, the hotel formed part of an ensemble of neo-Moorish, pro-Andalusian, *azulejo*-covered buildings constructed for the 1929 Ibero-American Exposition. A celebration of all things Spanish and Spanish-American, Expo '29 took some 15 years to build but ended in anti-climax: Seville was left with enormous debts. None of this worries the hotel's clientele, however; have a drink in the bar and admire its grand patio.

Continue along Calle San Fernando to the great hulk of the **Real Fábrica de Tabacos**, completed in 1757, and now part of Seville's University. It is possible to take a short-cut through the centre of the building, which still bears a few signs from the days when it employed thousands of young *cigarerras* to roll cigars. Some accounts suggest that 12,000 young girls worked here – the prospect clearly intoxicated the minds of many Romantic male travellers who came to Seville. One such was Prosper Mérimée, a French writer whose story about one of them, *Carmen*, inspired Bizet's opera.

If you walk through or round the building you'll arrive at a junction with a statue of the *Reconquista* hero El Cid. Skirt round

Plaza de España

it, past the Teatro Lope de Vega and into the Avenida Isabel la Católica. The towers of the **Plaza de España**, inspired by the cathedral at Santiago de Compostela, will guide you.

The enormous Plaza once housed the Spanish Pavilion but is now a nostalgic, *azulejo*-crazed playground. The rambling gardens of the **Parque de María Luisa** were once part of the grounds adjoining the baroque San Telmo Palace. Romantic statuary inhabits the undergrowth. Further south are two more pavilions in the Plaza de América (see 'Museums' itinerary).

When you've had enough cut through to the riverside Paseo de las Delicias, now a highway, where you can hail a taxi back.

2. La Maestranza and Reales Alcázares

To the bullring via the Archivo General de Indias. Inspect the paintings in the Hospital built by the original Don Juan. After a liquid lunch, lose yourself in the magnificent Reales Alcázares and gardens.

The centre of Seville is neatly split in two by the Avenida de la Constitución. To the east is the Cathedral and the Barrio Santa Cruz – the old Jewish quarter that was smartened up in the 1920s and has been metamorphosing into a picturesque tourist ghetto ever since. To the west lies El Arenal, a web of quiet, unpretentious streets centred on Seville's bullring, La Maestranza.

Before exploring this area, visit the **Archivo General de Indias** (open Monday–Friday 10am–1pm), in the heavyweight Lonja next to the cathedral. Formerly the stock exchange, the Lonja was designed in 1584 by Juan de Herrera, architect of Madrid's massive El Escorial. Since the 1750s it has been a records office for all the documents relating to the discovery and colonisation of the New World. A few of the thousands of millions of papers stored here are always out on display in the exhibition rooms up the grand stairs – perhaps a street-plan of Buenos Aires in 1713, a sketch of Inca weapons or a watercolour map of a fort in Florida.

From the Lonja cross over Avenida de la Constitución and turn right then left into Calle Almirantazgo. Here an archway to the right of the Café Los Pinelos will take you into the little-visited **Plaza del Cabildo**, the scene of a collectors' market on Sundays. Look for a small shop, El Torno, which sells delicious cakes and biscuits made by the various convents in and around Seville, and is a good place to buy something to nibble when you visit the Royal Palaces

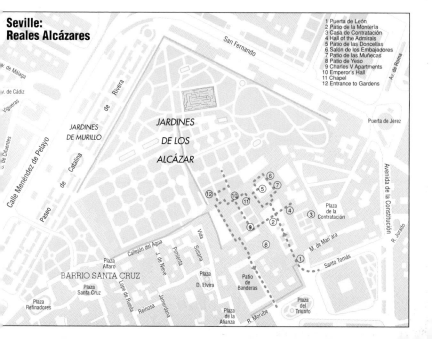

**Seville:
Reales Alcázares**

1 Puerta de León
2 Patio de la Montería
3 Casa de Contratación
4 Hall of the Admirals
5 Patio de las Doncellas
6 Salón de los Embajadores
7 Patio de las Muñecas
8 Patio de Yeso
9 Charles V Apartments
10 Emperor's Hall
11 Chapel
12 Entrance to Gardens

San Fernando

Av. de Reina

V. de Málaga

v. de Cádiz

Vigueras

de Rivera

JARDINES
DE MURILLO

JARDINES
DE LOS
ALCÁZAR

Puerta de Jerez

de Catalina

Calle Menéndez de Pelayo

de Cifuentes

Paseo

Avenida de la Constitución

Plaza
de la
Contratación

Callejón del Agua

Vida

Susana

Pimienta

J. de Nieve

M. de Mara

R. Jurado

Plaza
Alfaro

Lope de Rueda

BARRIO SANTA CRUZ

Plaza
Santa Cruz

Reinosa

Jamerdana

Plaza
D. Elvira

Patio
de
Banderas

Santo Tomás

Plaza
Refinadores

Plaza
de la
Alianza

R. Morube

Plaza
del
Triunfo

this afternoon. From here you can take a passage into Calle Arfe. Immediately in front of you is El Postigo, a municipal arts and crafts market.

Turn right, continuing down Calle Arfe and left into Calle Antonia Díaz. The junction of streets here is a good point to return to in the evening if you're looking for an easy-going place for dinner. Straight ahead is the popular Mesón Sevilla Jabugo II and

opposite a take-away *freiduría* (fried fish shop – only open evenings). Round the corner El Buzo and Bar Mesón Serranito both serve Sevillian dishes in a bullfighter's ambience. Heading back towards the cathedral, Bodegas Diaz Salazar in Calle García de Vinuesa is friendly and authentic.

At the bottom of Calle Antonio Díaz is La Maestranza – even if bullfighting isn't your cup of blood you have to admit that Seville's **Plaza de Toros** is an impressive piece of architecture (open 9.30am–2pm and 3–6pm). Built in 1760, it is one of the oldest and most prestigious bullrings in Spain. It's well worth taking a guided tour (30 mins), which in-

Arches in the Reales Alcázares

cludes a visit to its museum, matadors' chapel and stables. If you would like to attend a *corrida* then 'Bullfights' in the *Entertainment* section will tell you how.

From La Maestranza you can cross the road to the banks of the Río Guadalquivir, which was renamed the Canal de Alfonso XIII in 1948 when the river was diverted further west to prevent flooding. The river was re-opened for Expo '92, enabling visitors to cruise around the Isla de la Cartuja, the exhibition venue. Across the river to the north you'll see an iron bridge (built in 1852) crossing over to Triana, the traditional gypsy quarter of Seville. A blue-collar neighbourhood where most of Seville's dockers and watermen lived, Triana has a completely different atmosphere and is worth visiting to enjoy its shops and markets or its lively bars and nightlife.

The Torre del Oro

Turn left to walk down the pleasant Paseo de Cristóbal Colón. Ahead you will see the 13th century **Torre del Oro**, built by the Almohads to anchor a great chain that stretched across the river to defend the city. Today it contains a museum of nautical curiosities (Tuesday–Friday 10am–2pm, Saturday and Sunday 11am–2pm, closed Monday). From here you can take sightseeing bus tours of the city and cruises down the Guadalquivir.

Before you reach the tower cross back over the road and walk past the gardens of Seville's prestigious new opera house, the **Teatro de La Maestranza**, which opened in 1991 (Calle Nuñez de Balboa). At the end you will find the **Hospital de la Caridad** (Monday–Saturday 10am–1pm and 3.30–6pm). Founded in 1674, the building is still used as a charity hospital but is also open to the public. Apart from its exquisite patio, the Hospital has a chapel (to the left) that exemplifies the great patronage of the arts pursued by such institutions during Seville's Golden Age. Here you will find two ghoulish works by Valdés Leal (above the door and opposite) and several paintings by Murillo. Four of the best were pillaged by Marshal Soult in 1810.

Leaving the Hospital you will see a statue of its founder **Don Miguel de Mañara**, considered by some to be the role model for Don Juan, the cynical lover who had 1,003 Spanish mistresses. Decide for yourself if this man looks like a reformed seducer or a repentant Don Giovanni. The Hospital became a point of call for Romantic visitors who believed Seville to be the hot-bed of the lascivious South. Byron explained why in his own *Don Juan*: 'What men call gallantry, and gods adultery, / Is much more common where the climate's sultry.' Such contentious matters are best discussed over a glass of *fino*, which can be found in the cavernous **Bodegón Torre del Oro** round the corner (turn left into Calle Santander). If you like sherry this is a good place to taste some *manzanilla* or the stronger *oloroso*. The Bodegón also serves typical *raciones* such as *espinacas con garbanzos* (spinach with chick-peas) and *cola de toro* (bull's tail).

Suitably fortified, you now take on the **Reales Alcázares** (Monday to Saturday 10am–5pm, Sunday 2–6pm). The entrance to these Royal Palaces is in the Plaza del Triunfo to the east of the cathedral – straight up Calle Santander and Calle Santo Tomás. The Reales Alcázares are Pedro the Cruel's contribution to Seville's majestic monuments. For a Castilian king (1350–69) with a reputation for barbaric behaviour, it is surprising to find his palatial residences such a fulsome homage to the refined abstraction of Islam. Pedro, who adopted Arab dress and filled his court with Moorish entertainers, exemplifies how the Reconquest monarchs fell in love with what they had just destroyed. Ironically he had little time to enjoy his Alcázar – he was murdered three years after its completion.

You enter through the **Puerta de León** – close by are some castellated walls left over from the Almohad fortress that previously stood here. Inside you quickly discover that the Palaces have undergone considerable alteration since the 14th century. Passing through some small gardens you'll arrive in a large courtyard, the **Patio de la Montería**. Here you will find the work of Charles V, who added a whole set of **Royal Apartments** to the left. To the right is the **Casa de la Contratación**, the work of Ferdinand and Isabella, an establishment which had the monopoly on all trade with

Pavilion in the Alcázar gardens

Azulejo from the Emperor's Hall

the New World for over a century. Inside you'll find the **Hall of the Admirals** – used for planning naval expeditions – and beyond it a chapel with a starlit *artesanado* ceiling.

Ahead rises the exterior façade of Pedro's pleasure-dome. Inside (bear left) you pass through a vestibule to suddenly enter its opulent centre, the **Patio de las Doncellas** (Maids). Much of the Alcázar's decoration was probably executed by the craftsmen who worked on Granada's Alhambra; Seville's Christian rulers allowed them to incorporate Koranic inscriptions into the intricate tiles and stucco but had their own mottos and coats-of-arms added. The upper storey is a 16th century addition but the courtyard is still impressive – inevitably the *azulejos* steal the show.

Continuing straight ahead you enter the **Salón de Carlos V** with its fine coffered ceiling, followed by (turn right) three rooms that once belonged to Pedro the Cruel's mistress, María de Padilla. Turning the corner brings you into the **Salón de los Embajadores** (Ambassadors). The cedar cupola was added in 1427 and restored and embellished in subsequent centuries, but the room, with its triple arcade of horseshoe arches, is resoundingly Moorish. Parallel to this room is Philip II's dining room and ahead his bedroom – perhaps the sober wooden ceiling, such a contrast to the fireworks and starbursts elsewhere, was installed to help him get to sleep.

Next you enter the **Patio de las Muñecas** (Dolls) – apparently named after a pair of doll's heads in the decoration. The upper floor is a mid-19th century 'enhancement'. To the left is Isabella the Catholic's bedroom, and ahead that of her only son, Don Juan. To the right is the **Salón de los Reyes Moros** (Moorish Kings).

Back in the Patio de la Montería turn right towards an arcade. To the left of this you will find the oldest part of the Alcázar, including the **Patio de Yeso** that has survived from the 12th century Almohad palace. Continue through the gardens to the **Charles V Apartments** – first comes a room of Flemish tapestries depicting Charles's campaigns in Tunisia, followed by the Emperor's Hall and Chapel. Here the bright yellow *azulejos*, bursting with avaricious birds, snake-entwined cherubs and general Renaissance japery, make a refreshing change to the meditative geometrics of Islamic interior design. Their comic relief is an ideal introduction to the Alcázar's gardens that follow – a rambling paradise of box hedges and citrus groves mined with pools, pavilions and fountains, just the place to get lost in.

3. City Walk via Casa de Pilatos

This afternoon walk rambles through the some of the prettiest back streets of Seville, calling in at the very desirable Casa de Pilatos, an early 16th century palace that achieves a remarkable synthesis of Moorish and Renaissance spirits. It ends in Calle Sierpes, the city's principal shopping street. If you start at about 4pm on a weekday you should arrive in Sierpes when the 'paseo' is in full swing and its shops and cafés bubbling with life.

The walk starts in the **Patio de las Banderas** (Flags) – where you exit from the Reales Alcázares. An archway in the far corner will take you into the narrow streets of the **Barrio Santa Cruz**. After the covered alley bear left into Calle Vida. Leave via the long Callejón del Agua which ends in the Plaza de Alfaro: steps to the right lead down to the (**Jardines de Murillo**) Murillo Gardens. Continue ahead (bear left) into the Plaza de Santa Cruz, framed by Sevillian mansions with a 17th century iron cross in the centre. Further on, Calle Mezquita takes you to the Plaza Refinadores (Polishers), overseen by a haughty statue of Don Juan.

From the Callejón del Agua

Look for a small alley – Calle Mariscal – that will take you up to the Plaza de Cruces (Crosses), and another continuing straight on. At the top turn right into Calle Ximénez de Enciso, and when it ends go left towards the Hotel Fernando III for Calle Cespedes. This winds through to Calle Levies where you are confronted with a huge red-brick building (once a noble house, then convent and now a government building). Bear left into the Plaza de las Mercedarias, then take Calle Vidrio until it becomes pedestrianised, turning left (by No 25) into a tiny alley, the Calle Cristo del Buen Viaje. This delivers you to Calle San Esteban.

Turn left towards the restful **Plaza de Pilatos** where a statue of Zurbarán will greet you. If the great painter looks a bit annoyed it's probably because someone has stolen his paintbrush.

The **Casa de Pilatos** (daily 9am–6pm) is said to have been modelled on Pontius Pilate's house in Jerusalem by its creator, the Mar-

The Plaza de Cruces

quis of Tarifa. Completed in 1540, it is decorated in Mudéjar style but has none of the introversion and claustrophobia found in Pedro the Cruel's earlier Alcázar. Instead it is spacious and eclectic, a delightul combination of Italianate grace and Arab artistry. You enter first through a Roman-style triumphal arch, crossing the *apeadero* (carriage yard) to its central patio where arcades of Moorish arches are echoed by Gothic ones on the floor above.

This courtyard contains some of the finest *azulejos* you will ever see – dazzling, puzzle-book patterns in brilliant colours that include some extraordinary quasi-Impressionist designs. The Roman statuary was imported from Italy. If you walk to the right, through the Praetorian Chamber, you will discover a small garden. Continuing around the patio (in an anti-clockwise direction), you'll encounter the Chapel and Pilate's Study, which open onto enchanting gardens blessed with trickling fountains and cascading bougainvillea. A monumental staircase further round leads up to a late Mudéjar cupola (1537) that could have been inspired by a Ferrero Rocher chocolate. Here you can take a rather abrupt guided tour of the upstairs apartments, which are packed with art treasures acquired over the centuries by the palace's aristocratic owners (parts of the house are still used by the Medinaceli family).

When you leave, turn right to walk past the Hostal Atenas (Calle Caballerizas) to reach the ochre and amber façade of the Baroque Iglesia de San Ildefonso. Directly opposite is a brown metal door

Inside the Casa de Pilatos

Church of El Salvador

leading into the **Convento San Leandro**, a closed-order convent where you can buy – via a brass-studded revolving drum – its famous *yemas* (see 'Heavenly Sweets' in *Eating Out*).

Leave the adjacent plaza by the far corner, where Calle Boteros, then Calle Odreros, wind through to the **Plaza Alfalfa**, scene of an easy-going pet market on Sunday mornings. If you're ready for a snack, the **Horno San Buenaventura** patisserie is a must for anyone who considers cake-choosing a serious art form. From here you can follow the narrow Calle Alcaicería de la Loza (by the Carlos Antigüedades shop) into Seville's extensive pedestrian shopping area. First you will come across the Plaza de Jesús de la Pasión – devoted almost entirely to shops selling wedding dresses – and then the popular **Plaza del Salvador**. Between the two sits the fat church of El Salvador, built mostly in the 17th century.

The Plaza del Salvador sits half-way up a ladder of shopping streets running north-south. These are best explored at whim, but a good circuit is up to the top of Calle de la Cuna, left and then back down Seville's main strolling and spending artery, Calle Sierpes. While passing along Calle de la Cuna look out for the **Casa de la Condesa de Lebrija** (at No 8), another Sevillian stately home with a grand patio and stunning mosaics filched from Itálica (Monday and Friday only, 5–7pm; closed August).

At the top of Calle Sierpes La Campana (No 1) is one of the best cake shops in Seville if not in Spain. At the southern end of this serpentine street you will find the **Plaza Nueva** and the Plateresque façade of Seville's old **Ayuntamiento** (1564) – beyond this is the Avenida de la Constitución and the cathedral.

For dining consider the restaurants clustered around the north end of Calle Sierpes. Among these is **Las Columnas de Baco** (Calle Santa María de Gracia 2, Tel: 954 224320), useful if you want to escape the grime of the streets; if you eat at the bar it's a lot cheaper than at a table.

Back in the Plaza del Salvador the **Bar Alicantina** is famous for its seafood tapas, while on the opposite end of the square bars like La Antigua Bodeguita and Los Soportales cater to the younger crowd, who gather here for beer and food.

Street corner on Plaza Nueva

If you visit only one museum in your trip make sure it's the **Museo de Bellas Artes** (Plaza del Museo; Tuesday 3–8pm; Wednesday–Saturday 9am–8pm; Sunday 9am–2pm; closed Monday). For years it lay stranded in the unsalubrious streets bordering Seville's old railway station, Estación de Córdoba (now a shopping centre), and hardly helped its reputation by closing for interminable restoration. Expo '92 prompted the completion of this meticulous project and visitors can now visit one of the top fine art museums in the country. The building, constructed as the Convento de la Merced Calsada by Juan Oviedo in 1612, has three patios bordered by two floors of galleries exhibiting works chronologically from the medieval period to this century. The highlight is the main convent chapel with a baroque ceiling now so gloriously coloured it vies for attention with the great works below. The collection's strongest works are the Seville School's religious paintings and sculptures which were commissioned by the city's abundant and wealthy convents, monasteries and hospitals. The artists make an illustrious roll-call: El Greco, Pacheco, Velázquez, Cano, Zurbarán, Leal, Murillo... Other rooms offer insights into not-so-old Seville – vistas of the Guadalquivir with steamships docked beside the Torre del Oro and Gonzalo Bilbao's tribute to the ladies of the Tobacco Factory, *Las Cigarerras*, painted as recently as 1915.

If you have time, two more museums are worth considering, both down on the Plaza de América at the southern end of the Parque de María Luisa. The **Museo de Artes y Costumbres Populares** (open Tuesday 3–8pm; Wednesday–Saturday 9am–8pm; Sunday 9am–2pm, closed Monday) is housed in the Mudéjar Pavilion left over from the Ibero-American Exposition. A haphazard assemblage of Sevillian costumes, bedrooms, portraits and agricultural odds-and-ends, it nonetheless offers an enjoyable introduction to the traditions and clichés of 19th and 20th century Andalusia.

Opposite the museum stands the **Museo Arqueológico** (open Tuesday 3–8pm; Wednesday–Saturday 9am–8pm; Sunday 9am–2pm, closed Monday), housed in the Renaissance Pavilion. The highlight is the Tartessian Carambolo Treasure. The collection covers Neolithic to Moorish times, including Roman mosaics and statues from Itálica and Ecija. All these museums are free to EU citizens.

5. Churches

A long walk from the Plaza de Armas through the back streets of the Barrio Macarena – the 'Soul of Seville' – to the Basilica de Macarena, passing some of the city's finest churches.

The **Plaza de Armas** – being a bus terminus, a hotel and an underground parking lot seems an ideal place to begin a walk through one of Seville's most 'typical' neighbourhoods, showing the religious countenance of a city which was once the link between Europe and the Indies. In the centre of the plaza, the **Old Córdoba Train Station** (dating to 1889), is considered to be one of the most emblematic examples of Sevillian civic architecture. Its construction became a reference point for the future styles of regionalism and modernism which were soon to follow. Used as the Sevillian Pavilion during Expo '92, it is now an up-market commercial centre.

With the river at your back, walk to the next corner (Calle Marqués de Paradas) and turn right. When the road splits, bear left along Calle Julio César and continue until the Calle Reyes Católicos. Turn left; looking ahead the street narrows. If you let your eyes rise above the buildings you will catch a glimpse of the brightly coloured cupola of the church of **Santa Maria Magdalena**. It is difficult to see the building clearly because of the trees but it is worth looking for an angle to do so. If it is time for mass, (around 11am) go into the church and spend a few minutes contemplating the intricate labyrinth of paintings, frescos and altarpieces which adorn the interior.

Past the church, turn left onto Calle Bailén then right at the next small plaza which has more than its fair share of interesting buildings, into the shopping street Calle San Eloy. If it is sunny, stop for a coffee at the **Cafe Zafiro** (in the plaza) or, if not, a 'tapa' at the **Bar Rincon San Eloy** (number 30). Continuing to the end of the street, turn left into the small gardened square Plaza del Duque de la Victoria. On Thursday, Friday or Saturday a pleasant 'hippy market' is held here. You

The Old Córdoba Train Station, Plaza de Armas

Santa Maria Magdalena

can indulge in some more serious shopping in the unmissable El Corte Inglés department store or Marks and Spencer nearby. Leave the plaza with El Corte Inglés on your left and walk along Calle Jesús del Gran Poder, past the Plaza de la Concordia.

In front of the Farmacia Militar, turn right into Calle San Miguel then left when you reach Calle Amor de Dios, a street which seems to be an endless showcase of Sevillian urban architecture.

Immediately turn right into **Calle San Andrés** where you'll encounter the small Gothic church of **San Andrés**, which has constituent parts of many styles as well as Gothic. The patio at Calle Angostillo, 10 is worth looking into as well. Leave by Calle Cervantes, passing under the ceramic 'street chapel' of Nuestro Padre Jesús del Gran Poder. Ahead is the 14th-century Gothic church of **San Martín**. Also in the plaza are the pink 'palacete' and the interior patio of the modern white apartment building, worth noting as an example of just what can be done with a certain amount of good taste.

Leave the Plaza San Martín by way of Calle Viriato. One hundred metres along you arrive at the church of **San Juan de la Palma**, finished in 1788, in the style known as Gothic-Mudejar (with baroque bell tower). Note the unusual rectangular stained glass window over the entrance. To the right is a Renaissance facade of an old seignorial house which is now used as a shop.

From the plaza you can see the bell tower of the **Convento de Espíritu Santo**. Continue along the Calle San Juan de la Palma and follow the convent wall onto Calle Dueñas until you reach the entranceway of the **Palacio de las Dueñas**, a palace owned by the Duchess de Alba, who has more titles than the Queen of England. Un-

Sharpening on the street

37

Inside the Convent of Santa Paula

fortunately it isn't open to visitors but if the gate is open it is worth a peek into the garden.

Take Calle Doña Maria Coronel then the first left, Calle Gerona. If you're hungry (or still hungry), stop at the cafe El Rinconcillo at No 32 before arriving at the Mudéjar doorway of the church of **Santa Catalina**. Walk around the church anti-clockwise and note the Portal Gótico, which came from another church, the Mudéjar details and the tower.

After the complete circle, turn left towards the Plaza de los Terceros then keep right at the Libreria-Anticuaria **Los Terceros**. Fifty metres further along on the right is the 17th-century church of **Los Terceros**. The colonial baroque entrance is at the back of the church and dates from the 18th century.

The Virgin, a popular image in Andalusia

At the **Plaza de San Román** still another Gothic-Mudéjar church awaits. Take the left hand side of the church along Calle de Enladrillada. At the beginning of a long white wall turn left into Calle Santa Paula. At the plaza beyond is the **Convento de Santa Paula**. If you arrive during the posted visiting hours, knock on the right hand door. Shortly a nun will open and show you around the museum and offer to sell you some home-made sweets and marmalades. Knocking on the monumental 16th-century left-hand door will bring a guardian to show you around the church which, with its abundance of tiles and baroque details, is definitely worth a visit. Entrance to each is by a voluntary donation.

Leave the plaza by way of Calle Santa Paula (which becomes Calle Los Siete Dolores de Nuestra Señora). **Plaza Santa Isabel**, although at times dirty, is good place to sit and admire the Renaissance facade of the enormous church of the

Mudéjar window, San Marcos

Convento de Santa Isabel before taking a clockwise trip around the smaller Parochial Church of **San Marcos** beside the square. In Mudéjar style, with Renaissance additions, the church tower was once the minaret of a mosque. The fine Mudéjar window designs date back to before the founding of the church in the 14th century.

Facing the church's main door, turn left and follow Calle de San Luis. Soon you will see, on the left, the 3 doors of the **Iglesia de San Luis**. Dating back to 1699, it is one of the city's best examples of Sevillian baroque. If you're lucky and find it open, a look at the cupola is definitely worth the strain in the neck.

Continuing along Calle de San Luis you will pass the small church of **Santa Marina** to the right and later the **Parroquia de Gil** before arriving at the **Puerta de la Macarena**, the gate in the old Islamic walls.

A good finale to this route through the religious soul of Seville is a visit to the next-door **Basilica de la Macarena**. Dating back only to 1949, the basilica was built as a church-museum to house Seville's most beloved 'virgin' – **La Esperanza-Macarena**. For a small fee you can witness the orgy of devotion to the statue, which only leaves its pedestal once each year during Holy Week to be paraded through the streets under the adoring eyes of tens of thousands of the faithful.

Now you've deserved a rest and some refreshment. Across the road from the basilica is the **Bar Plata** or a short block to the north is a less expensive option, the **Hotel Macarena**, with a nice, well-appointed coffee shop.

6. The Legacy of Expo '92

Expo '92 left a lasting impression on Seville. Its most visible legacy is architectural. The site itself, on the island of Cartuja, still draws visitors with a range of attractions.

In 1992 Seville hosted the World Fair, Expo '92. The city was transformed and a whole new town of pavilions and exhibition spaces was built on a 450-acre (182-hectare) site on the island of Cartuja. The event attracted over 41 million visitors and put Seville back on the world map. The city is still reeling from the after-shocks of this grand project. Innovative bridges were built to span the Guadalquivir, notably the wishbone-shaped Puente de la Barqueta and the harp-like Puente del Alamillo. Seville gained a a re-vamped airport, a new railway station, roads and designer hotels.

A few of Expo's bold, hi-tech pavilions have survived on Cartuja. Some buildings now form part of a new Science and Technology Park, others are used by the city's university. The restored 14th-century Carthusian monastery, **Monasterio de Santa María de las Cueva** was the Royal Pavilion during Expo. (open Tuesday–Saturday 10am–8pm, Sunday 10am–3pm). Columbus stayed here often, and at one time was buried here. Between 1841 and 1980 the monastery housed the Pickman ceramic factory, famed for its Cartuja porcelain.

Part of the area next to the river has been incorporated into **Isla Mágica** (open March–October, all day), an 85-acre (34-hectare) theme park. Across the Puente de la Cartuja bridge is the **Puerta de Triana** recreation area, which incorporates Expo's Navigation Pavilion (exhibition of the history of ships and sailing), the Omnimax Space Cinema (360° wraparound cinema), the Observation Tower (bird's eye views of Seville) and a full-scale reproduction of the *Victoria*, the ship that first circumnavigated the world.

The **Estadio Olímpico** de La Cartuja was built as part of the city's unsuccessful bid to host the 2004 Olympic Games. The stadium hosted the 1999 World Athletics Championships.

Close encounter at the Isla Mágica

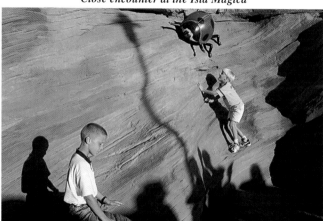

Córdoba hugs a lazy bend of the Guadalquivir at the southern foot of the Sierra Morena, 87 miles (140km) east of Seville. For a city endowed with such a glorious past – it was the capital of Roman Spain and later of al-Andalus – it has become surprisingly small and provincial. The city's enduring attraction is the vast, innovative mosque constructed by the Moors on the north bank of the river between the 8th and 11th centuries: La Mezquita – one of the wonders of the world. The old quarters of Córdoba fan out around this magnet, a compact warren of white-washed houses, winding alleys and flower-filled patios that generously reward the casual explorer. Beyond this sprawls the modern city where most of Córdoba's luxury hotels are located – but try if you can to stay in one of the several small hotels within the old quarter. If you haven't booked your accommodation ahead and can sacrifice comfort for character the area is well stocked with the cheaper *hostales* and *pensiones*, often with patios.

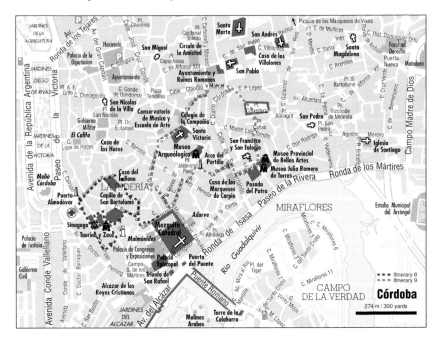

La Mezquita is best visited in the early evening when the sun has warmed its ancient stones and the school groups and armed guards have disappeared. Spend the morning exploring the old quarter or visiting the Alcázar or Palacio de Viana (Itinerary 7).

If you enjoy architecture allow a good two hours for contemplating the mosque and bring a jacket – it's cool inside! Before you enter, consider calling into **El Caballo Rojo**, the most famous restaurant in Córdoba, to book a table for dinner. Cardenal Herrero 28, Tel:

Spend the morning in the Alcázar (above), before going into the Mezquita

957 475 375) It specialises in *antigua cocina mozarabe*, traditional Córdoban dishes spiced and sweetened with Moorish flavours such as *cordero al miel* (lamb in honey) and *revuelto siglo XI* (scrambled egg *à la* 11th century).

Begin in the **Patio de los Naranjos**, which you can enter from either the east or west side of the Mezquita. Today it is an enclosed garden with bubbling fountains and lines of orange trees – an ideal place to sit and get your bearings. Construction of **La Mezquita** (open 10am–7pm summer, 5.30pm winter) began in AD785, 21 years after Abd ar-Rahman I, founder of the Umayyad dynasty, declared himself Emir of al-Andalus. Until then Córdoba's Moorish and Christian communities had shared a Visigothic church that originally stood here, San Vicente, which had simply been partitioned into two parts. After purchasing the Christian half the Moors constructed a new mosque – making extensive use of materials from the old church – which occupied roughly a quarter of the space of what you see today.

Over the next two centuries, as Córdoba's wealth and prestige grew, successive rulers enlarged and embellished this original structure, extending the mosque east and as far south as the Guadalquivir allowed. In 1236, when Ferdinand III captured Córdoba, the Mezquita

A Forest of Marble Palms

Palm trees, Arabian tents, Roman aqueducts, fans, acrobats on each other's shoulders ... theories abound as to what inspired the Mezquita's architects to create the innovative pillar-and-arch design that makes Córdoba's mosque such a thrill. What is readily apparent is that they began with a pile of assorted columns and capitals gathered from the earlier Visigothic church and from other plundered sources around al-Andalus. The builders may also have kept one of the Visigothic church walls in place – a possible explanation for the Mezquita's great mystery: why does the qibla, the prayer wall traditionally facing east to Mecca, actually face south?

These columns, all of differing height and stone, were ingeniously incorporated into the building – sunk into the ground, raised up, inverted – and then topped by other columns. Two tiers of arches, constructed of red brick and white plaster, then bridged the gap between them – the higher arch supporting the roof, the lower strengthening the grid of columns. The result is apparently top-heavy, but when repeated row upon row, it creates a momentum and harmony that is ultimately spacious and agile. Later architects elaborated on this basic form by interlacing and poly-lobing (an effect resembling a bite-mark) the arches. The result, built more than a thousand years before the visual conundrums of Escher or computer graphics, is stone magic.

reverted to Christian ownership: Catholic chapels were planted between its Roman and Visigothic pillars and many of its entrances blocked up. Over the course of the 16th century an extravagant cathedral was erected in its midst which earned a definitive rebuke from Charles V: 'You have built here something you could have built anywhere, but you have destroyed what was unique in the world.' This is rather ironic coming from an Emperor who made his own 'improvements' to the Alhambra and Seville's Alcázar and who himself sanctioned the work in the first place.

An appreciation of the Mezquita's former glory therefore requires some mental subtraction of Christian appendages. First remove all the filled-in arches along the mosque's northern wall, then open up all the closed doors in the walls surrounding the Patio; now lift off the 16th century bell-tower encasing the original minaret, swap the orange trees for olives, palms and cypresses and add a well and a waterwheel to the fountains.

In Arab cities a mosque is not a private religious compound but an integral part of the neighbouring streets – a combination of thoroughfare, meeting-place and, at the appointed hours, place of communal prayer. The Patio functioned as a courtyard for ritual ablution before prayer, the faithful being summoned by the wailing call from its slender minaret. Its main entrance would have been the **Puerta del Perdón** adjacent to this tower, which lies parallel to the principal entrance to the mosque, the **Puerta de las Palmas** (next to the four naves with wooden lattices).

Both were redecorated in Mudéjar style but the latter is still flanked by two Roman columns and a plaque inscribed in Arabic stating, just like an architect's signboard, that Said ben-Ayub had been commissioned to build the mosque by Abd ar-Rahman in year 346 of the Muslim calendar.

Mezquita doorway

Today you enter the hall of the mosque through a small door on the south-east corner of the Patio, at which point this book becomes superfluous. If you want more information the itinerary resumes in the far corner to your right (by the wooden lattices), but have a wander first.

If you can find enough light to read this, you will hopefully be near to a lonely Visigothic font that by the end of the day is usually full of empty film boxes. This corner of the Mezquita is the old, original rectangle built by Abd ar-Rahman I. Along the walls, rows of Catholic chapels stretch into the gloom. Remove these and you can imagine how the serried pillars within the mosque were a continuation of the trees back in the Patio de los Naranjos, part of a subtle transition from the mundane to the divine that culminates in the *mihrab*, the sacred niche in the prayer wall where the Koran is kept.

Walking ahead (anti-clockwise) you will move into the first extension of the mosque, obvious from a slight rise in the floor, added by Abd ar-Rahman II in 833. To the left is the back of the cathedral *coro*. Further on is the vaulted ceiling of an aborted attempt to build a church here in the 15th century. To the left is the domed **Capilla de Villaviciosa** where the old mosque's *mihrab* would have been. Through a cut-away you can see the **Capilla Real** next door, redecorated in the 14th century in Mudéjar stucco, which would have been the *maqsura* or royal enclosure of the mosque.

Continuing on you enter the Mezquita's **major enlargement**, a legacy of the golden days of 10th century Córdoba. This was built in 964 by al-Hakam II, son of the self-proclaimed Caliph Abd ar-Rahman III. He pushed the southern wall right up to the river and built a new opulent *mihrab*, decorated with dazzling mosaics and a star-ribbed dome that was subsequently copied throughout Spain. This lies beyond a set of railings – the bejewelled side-chambers formed

La Mezquita

1 St. Catherine's Gate
2 Dean's Gate
3 Patio de los Naranjos
4 Puerta del Perdón
5 Bell-Tower
6 Puerta de las Palmas
7 Entrance
8 Abd Ar-Rahman I's Original Mosque
9 Abd Ar-Rahman II's Extension
10 Villaviciosa Chapel
11 Royal Chapel
12 St. Paul's Chapel
13 Al-Hakam II's Extension
14 Mihrab
15 Sacristy
16 Al-Mansur's Extension
17 Transept
18 Choir
19 Chancel
20 St. Stephen's Door
21 St. Michael's Door
22 Palace Door
23 Virgin of the Lamps

C. Magistral González Francés

C. Torrijos

C. Cardenal Herrero

Moorish designs

the *maqsura*. Now so far away from the Patio, domed skylights had to be introduced here. Turning left you pass the cathedral sacristy and enter the **third extension** of the Mezquita, built by the belligerent al-Mansur in 990 to accommodate Córdoba's growing population. With the Alcázar to the west and the river to the south, his only option was to extend eastwards, widening both the hall and courtyard. Here the construction was conducted with more efficiency than artistry – the capitals of its uniform columns are less elaborate, the red is painted onto the arches – and probably reflects al-Mansur's greater interest in extending his caliphate, which reached as far as Santiago da Compostela.

Beside you stands the towering **Christian cathedral**, begun in 1523 and completed over the next two centuries. With its narrow aisles and lofty **Capilla Mayor**, designed to humble worshippers and direct their eyes to the heavens, it stands in marked contrast to the ubiquitous, unhierarchical Mezquita. It is nevertheless stunning, particularly the carved mahogany choir-stalls that fill the *coro* like some elaborate confection in dark chocolate.

Returning to the blinding light of the outside world, take the western exit from the Patio de los Naranjos and walk south towards the river. Here you will pass the richest of the Mezquita's **exterior façades**. The first doorway you meet (St. Stephen's) was the original entrance to the Visigothic church and Abd ar-Rahman I's original mosque. Next you pass the extension by Abd ar-Rahman II and another door (St. Michael's) that would have been a royal passageway from the Alcázar to the mosque's *maqsura*.

Three more entrances follow, all with brass-faced doors. These all date from the al-Hakam II period – the centre one, with its Gothic arch stuck like a pointed hat on top of the earlier Moorish horseshoe neatly encapsulates the spirit of architectural one-upmanship that has created the Mezquita you see today. Everywhere historical interest is gained at beauty's expense – a truth borne out further when you reach the Mezquita's south-western corner. Here you will find an absurd collision of Time's left-overs – a Roman bridge, a 16th century triumphal gate built by Philip II and an 18th century monumental column to St Raphael. For much of the day these are strangled by an endless string of cars, horse-drawn carriages and tourist buses. Once the Mezquita closes, however, the city suddenly relaxes – a cathartic moment, and an ideal time to walk out across the Puente Romano. Pause beside the silty waters of the Guadalquivir and, like so many before you, contemplate Córdoba in the fading sunlight, before preparing yourself for dinner.

Horse-drawn carriages outside the Mezquita's Palacio Episcopal

8. Exploring the Judería

Córdoba's old Jewish quarter, the Judería, lies to the northwest of the Mezquita, and can be explored in a couple of hours.

A Sephardim community has been here since Roman times: subsequent persecution by the Visigoths forced its members to side with the invading Moors and as a reward for their support the Jews were allowed to remain in the city. For seven centuries they lived in fruitful co-existence with Córdoba's tolerant Muslim rulers until their expulsion by Ferdinand and Isabella in 1492.

The quarter is now an easy-going maze of narrow streets where craft shops and souvenir stalls are gradually infiltrating its smarter residences and neglected historic buildings. Start in the **Calle Cardenal Herrero** and walk west towards a T-junction of *souk*-like streets where you can pick up an ice cream at Helados Alberti to help keep your fellow pedestrians at bay. Take Calle Deanes (sharp right), past No 16 which has an above-average selection of the *filigrana de plata* (silver filigree) for which Córdoba has long been famous. Cassettes of flamenco and guitar music can be bought around here.

At the end of the street turn left into Calle Buen Pastor which curls uphill to the Plaza Angel Torres. Nearby is the **Casa del Indiano**, a misleading title for a 15th century Mudéjar-style gate. Walk past this till you reach the more substantial **Puerto Almodóvar**, part of the Moorish city walls. If you turn left beyond this (after bowing to the statue of Seneca), you can follow a pleasant, pool-lined promenade that runs beside the walls. At the end you'll meet a statue of the 12th century philosopher, medical writer and commentator on Aristotle, Averroës – one of the most famous thinkers of Córdoba's golden age. Near here an arch in the walls re-admits you to the Judería.

A sinuous alley (Calle La Luna) leads to a crossroads where you turn left (Calle Tomás Conde) into the Plazuela Maimónides. Here the **Museo Municipal de Arte Taurino** (open 8.30am–2.30pm in summer; 10am–6pm in winter; closed Sunday afternoon and Monday) is dedicated to the art of bullfighting. Continue past a statue of Maimónides, a 12th-century Jewish scholar and philosopher whose treatises on medicine were translated throughout medieval Europe. To your right you will find the **Zoco**, a handicrafts market with studios and workshops selling high-quality Córdoban leather goods, jewellery and ceramics. Further on (Calle Judios) you'll encounter one of Spain's three surviving **synagogues** (the other two are in Toledo). It is remarkable that this small, intimate place of worship still exists: it dates from 1314 and has walls bearing Mudéjar ornament and Hebraic inscription. Over the centuries it has served as a hospital for rabies victims, hermitage, cobbler's, school and warehouse before being rescued (open 10am–2pm, 3.30–5.30pm, 10am–1.30pm Sunday, closed Monday.)

After the synagogue turn right into Calle Averroës which will take you round the back of the Zoco, past the beautifully dilapidated church of San Bartolomé and (left at No 5) into the Plaza del Cardenal Salazar. Here the busy restaurant **El Churrasco** specialises in grilled meats (*churrasco* is a grilled pork dish with pepper sauce) and has a good selection of *tapas* (Calle Romero 16, tel: 957 290819). From here Calle Romero will take you back to the Mezquita. **Taberna Pepe de la Judería** at the bottom, despite its hectic location, is a friendly bar and restaurant, good for a quick coffee or a slow lunch. If you want to escape the tour groups try **La Fragua**, up an alley at the bottom of Calle Tómas Conde.

9. City Walk and Museums

This half-day itinerary takes you to the less-visited eastern part of Córdoba where the old city intermingles with the new. Venture out in the morning if you like markets and shopping, in the afternoon if you enjoy the peace of empty streets.

Start in **Calle Cardenal Herrero** and walk east to its junction with Calle Magistral González Francés, where you can walk up the narrow Calle Encarnación. **Taller Meryan** at No 12 is a workshop with a typical range of traditional Córdoban tooled and embossed leather goods for sale. A quintessential part of Córdoba's character which you will encounter frequently in this walk is the patio. These inner courtyards were built by the Moors as cool central sanctuaries where their owners could escape the fierce heat of the summer. They often have a central fountain encircled by ferns with the surrounding walls bedecked with brightly-flowering pot-plants, patterned ceramic plates and cheerful *azulejos*.

Turn right, then left by the Hostal La Milagrosa (Calle Horno del Cristo) into the **Plaza del Jerónimo Páez**. This contains the province's **Museo Arqueólogico**, housed in a Renaissance palace (open Tuesday 3–8pm; Wednesday–Saturday 9am–8pm; Sunday 9am–3pm; closed Monday). Take the pedestrian Calle Julio Romero de Torres which winds round (past No 19) to descend the Calle del Portillo. At the bottom an ancient archway takes you beyond the old city walls – opposite is the Baroque Convento de San Francisco. Turn right, cross the road, then take the second left to pass the Hostal Maestre (Calle Romero Barros), which delivers you into the charming **Plaza del Potro**.

The plaza gets its name from the *potro* (foal) soaring above its gushing 16th-century fountain. A plaque nearby immodestly reminds visitors that Cervantes mentioned the square 'en la mejor novela del mundo' ('the best novel in the world'). *Don Quixote*'s creator stayed in its *posada* (inn), now an arts centre which contains a permanent exhibition (free entry) of *guadamecí* – a style of embossed and coloured leatherwork introduced to Córdoba from North Africa in the 9th century.

Opposite is the **Museo Provincial de Bellas Artes** (open Tuesday 3–8pm; Wednesday–Saturday 9am–8pm; Sunday 9am–3pm; closed Monday), housed in the former Hospital de la Caridad. It contains an agreeable miscellany of Córdoban *objets trouvés* including Roman relics, religious portraits, prints of old Córdoba, one Goya

Córdoban patio

engraving, some 20th century sculpture. Also inside is the **Museo Julio Romero de Torres**, devoted to a local painter (1880–1930) responsible for the sultry and (to male Spanish eyes) erotic portraits of under-dressed Andalusian women.

At the top of the Plaza del Potro, a small street (past No 15) takes you past a puppeteers' workshop and turn right round into Calle Armas. Head straight on via Calle Sanchez Peña to reach the large rectangular **Plaza de la Corredera**. A traditional site for the city's markets, bullfights and entertainments, the galleried brick buildings enclosing the square were built in 1688. Today it is the scene of an easy-going market, selling clothes, crafts and an assortment of household items.

Further on you will see the restored columns of a Roman temple standing somewhat bizarrely next to the modern Ayuntamiento. If you intend to visit the **Palacio de los Marqueses de Viana** (open 9am–2pm in summer; 10am–1pm and 4–6pm in winter; Sunday

Puppeteers' workshop by Plaza del Potro

10am–2pm; closed Wednesday and 1–15 June), turn right here. This is a 16th-century Córdoban stately home which was in private ownership until 1980. With no fewer than 13 patios and 38 rooms and galleries crammed with antiques collected from all over the world, it is guaranteed to trigger the imagination. Whirlwind guided tours only.

Back on the walk, continue uphill along Calle Claudio Marcelo. This culminates in Córdoba's bus-clogged central square, the **Plaza de las Tendillas**, but you will find life quieter if you turn left by the Ferreteria Central – which does a good line in hand-made calf-skin working boots – into a pedestrianised shopping precinct (Calle Conde de Cárdenas).

Walking through you will discover the 16th century Jesuit church **Salvador y Santo Domingo**, a monument to St Raphael (a civic obsession) and further ahead the curved façade of the 18th century **Iglesia de Santa Victoria**. Skirting this to the violin strains that often emanate from the Music Conservatory in Calle Juan Valera, you reach a main street (Calle Angel de Saavedra) where you turn left to head downhill along Calle Blanco Belmonte towards the Mezquita. There is a good view of its tower from the Plaza Benavente. Take a small alley to the left of this plaza (past No 2) which will lead you to Calle Velazquez Bosco. This runs down to the Mezquita: on the way take a trip up the **Calleja de las Flores**, the vainest, most-photographed street in Córdoba.

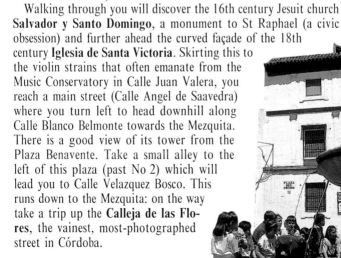

Plaza del Potro

GRANADA

Only 50 miles (80km) from the Mediterranean coast, Granada stands a cool 2,247ft (685m) above sea level. Once stacked up around three foothills of the **Sierra Nevada** – Albaicín, Sacromonte and Alhambra – the city now oozes out over the eastern end of the *vega*, the long fertile plain which in Moorish times was a vast market garden full of orchards, farms and watermills. Further east rise the mountains of the Sierra Nevada, their snowy peaks providing the waters for the two principal rivers that weave through the city, the Darro and the Genil.

Granada's famous Alhambra can absorb as much of your time as you care to give it. Spare a few hours for exploring the cobbled streets of the Albaicín too: once a separate walled Moorish city, it has yet to succumb to the prettification that similar old quarters in Seville and Córdoba have undergone. Modern-day Granada, as you will discover unless you are fortunate enough to be staying in the ethereal surroundings of the Alhambra hill, is hectic, polluted and relentlessly persecuted by traffic. However, it has a lively university and a good programme of cultural activities.

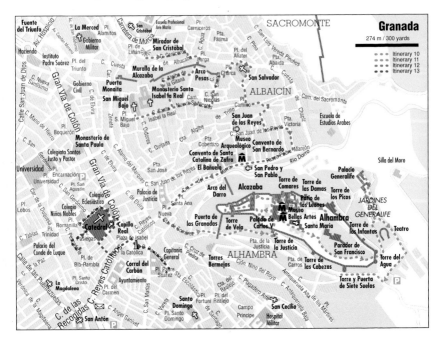

Plan an entire day to explore the wonders that await on the Alhambra hill, taking your time to visit the different sections: the Alcazaba fortress, the Generalife gardens, the renaissance Palace of Charles V and the exquisite Nasrid Palaces.

To make the most of your visit to the different parts of the Alhambra, it is crucial that you obtain your ticket in advance (see page 56). Your ticket will show your admission time to the Nasrid Palaces; structure the rest of your tour – the Alcazaba, Generalife, Palace of Carlos V – around that time. Here we're assuming you have time to spare and will save the Nasrid Palaces for last.

The traditional approach to the Alhambra involves a steep, half-hour walk up from the Plaza Nueva. The ascent soon discards the grimy shops of the Cuesta de Gomérez in favour of the cool woods of the Alhambra hill, passing through the **Puerta de las Granadas**

Puerta de las Granadas

(Gate of the Pomegranates – the city's emblem) and (take the left hand path) delivering you outside the citadel's most imposing entrance, the **Torre de la Justicia**. As you wind through this great Moorish gateway two symbols above its horseshoe arches remind visitors that they are entering the world of Islam: a hand (representing the faith's five tenets: the oneness of God, prayer, fasting, alms-giving and pilgrimage) and a key (representing the power Allah gave the Prophet to open and close the gates of heaven).

If you prefer to arrive by taxi or by bus (every 15 minutes from Plaza Nueva), just follow the signs here. Whichever way you come, you'll confront the massive bulk of **Charles V's** decidely un-

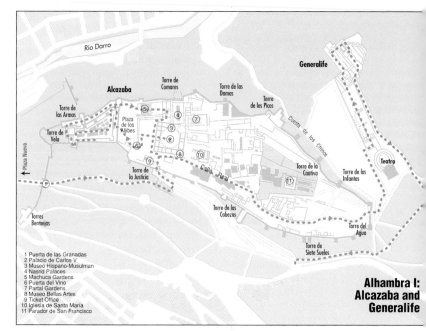

**Alhambra I:
Alcazaba and
Generalife**

Moorish **palace**, commissioned in 1526 but built almost a century later. Visit it first (admission free), for its stark and haughty Renaissance grandeur contrasts informatively with the frenzied eggbox ceilings and crazy-stuccoing you will see later in the Nasrid Palaces. The design – by Pedro Machuca – is a masterpiece and sadly his only surviving work. Once within its inner courtyard you will immediately appreciate the simplicity and power of the architect's concept – a circle in a square, executed in unadorned stonework.

To the left of the courtyard is the **Museo de la Alhambra** (open Tuesday to Saturday 9am–2.30pm only). It is worth visiting, if

The Alhambra's Court of the Myrtles

only to see the famous **Jarrón de la Alhambra**, a 14th century Nasrid vase decorated with gazelles and as good a definition of beauty as any. The collection contains many relics from the Alhambra's glory days: ceramics, *azulejos*, pottery lamps, carved roof-beams, marquetry chessboards, even a copper minaret – all of which will help you bring this great Moorish stage set to life. Opposite the museum's exit is the **Museo Bellas Artes** (open Tuesday 2.30–8pm; Wednesday–Saturday 9am–8pm; Sunday 9am–2.30pm, closed Monday): if you push on through its worthy collection of religious paintings and sculpture you'll find the 19th century galleries have an entertaining display of coy and picaresque characters from Romantic Andalusia.

After collecting some almonds or hazelnuts from the sweet-seller back by the entrance, continue through the **Puerta del Vino** towards the battlements of the Alcazaba. This is the oldest part of the fortress – some sections date from the 9th century but the two towers overlooking the Plaza de los Aljibes (Cisterns) are 13th century. Their burnt red walls (*al-Hamra* is Arabic for 'the red') remind us that the Alhambra began life as a military garrison. The plaza you are crossing was once the moat, then an underground cistern, and now, appropriately, contains a kiosk selling drinks.

You enter the **Alcazaba** by the Torre Quebrada (Broken Tower) and pass around the the Torre del Homenaje (Homage Tower) to

The Tale of the Alhambra

Construction of the Alhambra began in 1238 at the behest of Ibn-al-Ahmar, founder of the Nasrid dynasty. He rebuilt the ancient fortress of the Alcazaba, originally separated from the main hill by a ravine (now the Plaza de los Aljibes) and diverted the waters of the Darro to supply the new citadel. Most of the palatial splendour you see today was built in the 14th century by craftsmen who fled here as al-Andalus shrivelled with the Reconquest.

The Catholic Monarchs Ferdinand and Isabella admired the palaces and even restored parts of them. They installed a cathedral within the mosque (replaced in the late 16th century by the Iglesia de Santa María) and built the Franciscan convent (now the Parador). Their grandson Charles V was more heavy-handed, demolishing more than he replaced and plonking his imperial palace down on the site of the cemetery. With the expulsion of the Moors, along with some minor earthquakes and a gunpowder explosion in 1590, the Alhambra fell into decline.

Some two centuries later the Alhambra was ransacked by Napoleon's troops. This parlous state of decay ultimately proved beneficial, for it endeared the Alhambra to the Romantic writers, artists and travellers then discovering (some would say inventing) the exotic Spain of the 19th century. 'The Alhambra,' Benjamin Disraeli declared in 1830, 'is the most imaginative, the most delicate and fantastic creation that ever sprang up on a Summer night in a fairy tale.' Such eulogistic appreciation of this clapped-out castle goes a long way to explaining why we are all gathered here today.

By 1870 the Alhambra had been declared a national monument and today it is on UNESCO's list of World Heritage sites. Your gratitude to the Romantics who rediscovered it should be expressed by purchasing a copy of *Tales of the Alhambra* (on sale everywhere), written by an American diplomat, Washington Irving, who lived here for a few months in 1829, and by doing a bit of dreaming yourself.

Visiting the Alhambra

Visitors to the Alhambra are restricted to 7,700 per day. Tickets have three parts: the Alcazaba and Generalife can be visited at any time during the day, but you must enter the Nasrid Palaces during the half hour time slot shown on the ticket (though there is no limit on the time you spend there once inside). Admission to the Palace of Carlos V is free and unrestricted.

Tickets can sell out very quickly. To avoid disappointment, **purchase yours in advance** by ringing Linea BBV (up to one year ahead): on 902 22 44 60 (from Spain) or 34 913 745 454 (from abroad); or buy direct from BBV banks in Spain. To buy on the day, go early and expect queues. The ticket office is located at the bottom of the car park.

Be careful not to miss your slot for entering the Nasrid palaces. A complete tour involves walking almost 2 miles (3.2 km), but this vast walled garden filled with historical delights should not be hurried through. Come equipped for indolence: take a book big enough to snooze under, a stack of unwritten postcards, a bag of cherries.

If you are fortunate enough to be in Granada on a Tuesday, Thursday or Saturday, visit the Nasrid Palaces at night, open 10–12pm (in winter, Saturday only 8–10pm; same procedure for tickets). At such times the Alhambra's magic becomes palpable.

reach the Plaza de Armas – which would have once been filled with houses and barracks. Today only the dungeons and cisterns are visible. On its far side signs guide you towards the main tower, the **Torre de Vela** (Watchtower). On the way be sure to enjoy the little-visited **Jardín de los Adarves** with its classic terrace view of the Sierra Nevada. There are yet better views from the top of the Torre de Vela: for centuries its bell was used to tell the farmers of the *vega* when to irrigate their crops.

The Alhambra's one-way system directs you next down beside the battlements and out to the Machuca Gardens. The entrance to the **Nasrid Palaces** follows, but leave that for later if time permits. Instead make your way back to the Palacio de Carlos V and around into the centre of the Alhambra precinct. Here the Calle Real leads up past the Iglesia de Santa María to the **Restaurante Polinario**, which offers a satisfying buffet for a reasonable price. Further on is the luxury **Parador de San Francisco**, a former convent dating from 1495.

To the right of the Parador is the entrance to the **Generalife**. This was the Nasrid rulers' summer residence, created in the mid-13th century and re-created today as a horticultural paradise inspired by Moorish themes. The gardens incorporate many features similar to those you will find in the palace buildings – hidden entrances, enclosed gardens, pools and fountains – only here their intention is the creation of delight. Towards the end of the Generalife are some restored pavilions with views to Sacromonte hill.

To leave the gardens, an avenue of oleanders nearby leads to the eastern exit. From here you can drift back down (beech avenues) back into Granada through the verdant Alamedas.

View from the Alcazaba

The Nasrid Palaces constitute the inner sanctum of the Alhambra. Beyond the palaces lie some idyllic gardens and patios, so plan to spend some time here.

The entrance lies to the far side of the Palacio de Carlos V. The first room you enter is the **Mexuar**, an audience chamber used for judicial and administrative business. In the 18th century it was converted into a chapel – the *azulejos* are from Seville, and in Moorish times there would have been a cupola and lantern rather than the present carved wood roof. At the end is the **Oratory**, from which there is the first of many fine views out over the Albaicín and Sacromonte hills.

Another reception area follows, the **Golden Room**, decorated in Mudéjar style after the Reconquest. Opposite it is the **Mexuar Patio** (which would make an excellent squash court), and the façade of the Comares Palace. Here you can study the intricate patterns of the plasterwork, constructed in low relief to catch the sunlight, that was used to decorate many of the palaces' walls. Islam proscribes the depiction of the human form and the Alhambra's craftsmen vigorously pursue the abstract: the intention is to direct the eye to the infinite and the mind to the divine by a rhythmic dazzle of repeated floral shapes, interlocking geometric forms, multi-centred grids and ribbons of Koranic inscription joined together to proclaim the oneness of God.

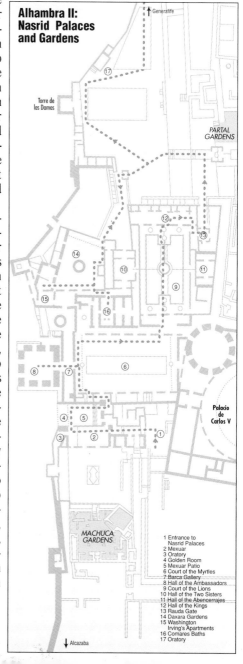

Alhambra II: Nasrid Palaces and Gardens

Generalife

Torre de las Damas

PARTAL GARDENS

Palacio de Carlos V

MACHUCA GARDENS

1 Entrance to Nasrid Palaces
2 Mexuar
3 Oratory
4 Golden Room
5 Mexuar Patio
6 Court of the Myrtles
7 Barca Gallery
8 Hall of the Ambassadors
9 Court of the Lions
10 Hall of the Two Sisters
11 Hall of the Abencerrajes
12 Hall of the Kings
13 Rauda Gate
14 Daxara Gardens
15 Washington Irving's Apartments
16 Comares Baths
17 Oratory

Alcazaba

The Partal Gardens

Once you take the small passage leading into the **Court of the Myrtles** two further principles followed by the Alhambra's architects become apparent: the desire to create awe-inspiring histrionic effects (with bland exteriors and concealed entrances for example), and the concern to make natural elements, particularly light and water, an integral and active part of the architecture. Now you are in the Serallo, the heart of the royal palace where foreign emissaries would have been received. As you skirt the long goldfish pond (clockwise) you pass a small niche that allows close inspection of the stalactital stuccowork. The faded colours still caught in its recesses remind us that such ornamentation, only made from a crude assemblage of brick, wood and plaster, was once painted and gilded.

Next you pass through the Barca Gallery, an ante-chamber to the splendid **Hall of the Ambassadors** where the Moorish Kings presided. Be sure to take a seat here so you can contemplate its impressive domed ceiling, a celestial cosmos of inlaid wood depicting the seven heavens revolving around the seat of God.

Continue around the Court of the Myrtles and through a small passage leading into the *harem*, the private section of the palace

Stuccowork in the Nasrid Palaces

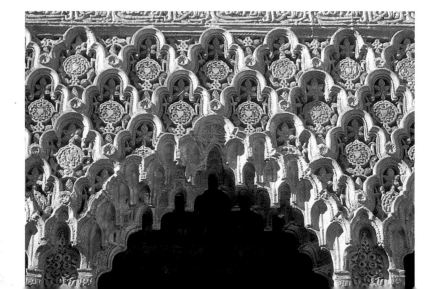

and also the last to be built. It is heralded by the famous **Court of the Lions**, which some feel to be the decadent swansong of a doomed monarchy. The design represents a symbolic Islamic paradise: an enclosed garden (substitute plants for what is now gravel) with a central fountain from which the four rivers of paradise flow into four restful pavilions surrounded by a forest of marble palms. Around the fountain stand 12 lions, perhaps representing the 12 signs of the zodiac or the tribes of Israel.

Here, and in the adjacent four rooms, the Sultan and his entourage resided: to the left as you enter are his wife's apartments (**Hall of the Two Sisters**) with a cupola said to have over 5,000 cavities. Opposite this is the **Hall of the Abencerrajes**, used for entertainments, with an octagonal ceiling resembling the rear-view of a just-launched rocket. Ahead is the **King's Hall** with alcoves behind that were once bedchambers. The ceilings above these are leather and painted with scenes of courtly life, presumably executed by a Christian artist under Moorish commission.

The exit from the palaces leads through the ivy-clad **Rauda Gate** into the **Partal Gardens** (formerly the servant's quarters and vegetable plots), where a kiosk nearby offers the welcome chance for a cool drink. Later you can wander down the terraces and left to the Lindaraja and Daxara Gardens, both former apartments of the harem that were remodelled in the 16th century. It was in this secluded corner of the Alhambra that Washington Irving lived in 'delicious thraldom' while he wrote his bestseller. Here you will also discover the damp, tiled chambers and star-spangled domed roofs of the **Baño de Comares**, the Royal Baths – the most evocative part of the complex.

Returning to the Partal Gardens you will pass a pavilion built above the fortress walls and faced by a pool guarded by two lions said to have been rescued from the lunatic asylum that occupied part of the Alhambra in the mid-19th century. Nearby is a small Moorish oratory while further on a string of ancient towers and modern gardens lead up towards the Generalife.

Into the gardens

12. Exploring the Albaicín

Piled up on a steep hill facing the Alhambra, the Albaicín was the heart of Moorish Granada and seat of the royal court for two centuries before the Nasrids built their palaces on the opposite side of the Darro river. When the city fell to Ferdinand and Isabella in 1492 the Albaicín had 60,000 inhabitants; by the start of the 17th century the persecution and expulsion of the rebellious 'moriscos' (Muslim converts) had reduced this to 6,000.

Traditionally a poor quarter, the Albaicín is now a pleasant, unpretentious maze of narrow streets lined with whitewashed houses, high-walled palaces and neglected churches and convents. Despite the gentrification seeping through the alleys, its Moorish character persists, the air still delicately perfumed with jasmine and mule dung. Head up here around midday for a late lunch and stroll: you can climb up from the **Plaza Nueva** but it is heavy going – it is a lot more advisable to take a taxi or a No 12 bus (from Calle Acera de Darro, near to Galerías Preciados) up to the **Mirador de San Cristóbal**.

From this Mirador there is a fine view over Granada and the *vega*: in the foreground you will see the old city walls of the Albaicín. From here you can take Calle Brujones (to the left of a souvenir shop) and turn right to descend a steep cobbled street (Cuesta de San Cristóbal). Soon you will pass two recurring features of the Albaicín: to the left an *aljibe* (water cistern), to the right a *cármen* or private walled house and garden.

Drop down the hill into the Plaza Almona, then go left up into the **Plaza Larga**. This is the hub of the Albaicín – in the morning a market, for the rest of the day an open-air café and meeting place. In the right-hand corner of the plaza stands the 11th century **Puerta Nueva** with a defensive dog-leg passage. After passing through the gateway, continue straight through the Placeta de las Minas, then turn right into Calle Aljibe de la Gitana. After a turn to the left you arrive at the small park – the Placeta del Cristo de las Azucenas. This adjoins two of the Albaicín's best known buildings – the moorish palace of **Dar al-Horra** and the **Monasterio Santa Isabel la Real** (1501).

Here you can either turn right toward the palace or continue

Aljibe in the Albaicín

Plaza San Miguel Bajo

down the slope and turn right on Calle Isabel la Real to go to the monastery. Both routes lead to the quiet **Plaza San Miguel Bajo**, a good place to stop for a drink or a light lunch. Bar Lara offers meats from the Alpujarras. From the Plaza return along the Camino Nuevo de San Nicolás, where a curve to the left will lead you up some steps to the Mirador de San Nicolás and a postcard-perfect view of the Alhambra. Ahead you can see the old city walls running across Sacromonte hill, along with the abandoned caves of Granada's old gypsy quarter. Descend the steps and turn right to reach a small plaza beside the Iglesia del San Salvador.

From here you can zig-zag your way downhill by any route that keeps you facing the Alhambra. Following the signs to the **Cármen-Restaurante Mirador de Morayma** (1.30–3.30pm, 8.30–11.30pm, closed Sunday, Tel: 958 228290) is a good option, leading you to one of Granada's most delightful restaurants: not only does it offer the rare chance to get inside a flower-filled *cármen,* it also serves local specialities like *espinacas al Sacromonte* and *habas con jámon*, along with Sierra Nevada cheeses. An easy route down from here is via Calle Placeta de Toqueros, where you turn left then right to descend the gentle gradient of the Cuesta de la Victoria. Now you are beside the Darro ravine. The plaza here has a gentle neighbourhood atmosphere – worth returning to in the evening when it becomes a mix of café-dawdlers, basketball-players and baked potato-sellers. A range of bars along the **Paseo del Padre Manjón** serve *tapas* and small dishes – La Fuente plays good Spanish pop music.

From here you can follow the Darro back towards the city centre along a narrow, traffic-constipated street. On the way you will pass the Casa del Castril, home of the **Museo Arqueológico** (Tuesday to Saturday 10am–2pm), and **El Bañuelo** (No 31, open Tuesday–Saturday 10am–2pm) housing well-preserved 11th-century Arab public baths with domed roofs and star-shaped vents.

Beside the river Darro

13. Morning Walk in the Cathedral Quarter

You could quite easily pass through Granada without even noticing it had a cathedral. Lost in a huddle of nondescript buildings below the Gran Vía de Colón, it is built on the site of the city's main mosque, a Christian spaceship rocketed into the heart of Muslim Granada. The surrounding district bears witness to this mixed heritage, a patchwork of pedestrian shopping streets and leafy plazas that is liveliest in the mornings.

Tombs of Ferdinand and Isabella in the Capilla Real

The **Plaza de Bib-Rambla**, just west of Calle Reyes Católicos, is a pleasant starting point. Once the site of a great Moorish gate, its pavement cafés are a good spot to sit and watch Granada wake up. Close to these cafés Calle Pescadería will lead you into Granada's central market area, a sprawl of stalls that adjoin the covered **Mercado Municipal de San Agustin**.

From the centre of Calle Pescadería the short Calle Marqués de Gerona, a street devoted to knife-sellers, will take you to the Plaza de las Pasiegas. After several false starts, construction of Granada's **cathedral** (daily 10.30am–1pm, 4–7pm; closed Sunday morning) began in 1523 and employed a procession of famous artists: here you see its main façade, designed in 1667 by Alonso Cano. Skirt left around the building, past two portals by the cathedral's principal architect, Diego de Siloé, and along Gran Vía de Colón until you discover the entrance, inevitably mobbed by carnation-sellers.

The **interior** of the cathedral, which was not completed until 1714, is cavernous and rather austere. A *retablo* dedicated to Saint James (left as you enter) clamours for attention, as does Siloé's domed Capilla Mayor – half way up its central arch are two statues of Ferdinand and Isabella kneeling in prayer. Curiously the

Lead coffins in the crypt

small **museum** (at the opposite end) and the intimate **sacristy** (right as you enter) are of more interest: the first contains a giant monstrance paraded through the streets at Corpus Christi, the second some elegant Parisian chests-of-drawers and a friendly Ellicot 'Strike Silent' grandfather clock.

When you leave the cathedral turn right into Calle Oficios and the **Capilla Real** (daily 10.30am–1pm, 4–7pm; closed Sunday afternoon), resting place of Ferdinand and Isabella. Once again the side-shows prove the best attractions: first you encounter the sacristy (the usual point of entry, via the Lonja, is closed for restoration), rich with regal art and treasures. Push on through to the chapel itself, where the marble tombstones (1517) of Ferdinand and Isabella (nearest as you enter, their actual remains in the crypt below) are upstaged by the larger ones of Philip the Fair and Joan the Mad, placed there by their son, Charles V. The chancel is fronted by a wrought-iron grille, and nearby hangs a triptych by Dierick Bouts. You'll find more Flemish masters in the sacristy, including works by Memling, van der Weyden and Botticelli.

Back in Calle Oficios you'll pass the site of Granada's Arab university, **La Madraza**, founded in 1349 by Yussuf I and now part of Granada University – if the door is open you can inspect a small, richly-decorated oratory across the patio, only uncovered in 1893. Carrying on down the street and left through a small arch, you will enter the Alcaicería, a 19th century reconstruction of the Arab silk market that originally stood here. Today it is a repetitive parade of souvenir stalls. If you continue straight on you can cross Calle Zacatin, a long pedestrian shopping street, to reach Calle Reyes Católicos. Directly across the road in Calle Lopez Rubio you will see a horseshoe arch marking the entrance to the **Corral del Carbón**. This was once a 14th century caravanserai where merchants and their animals were quartered. Inside is a central courtyard surrounded by three-storeyed galleries: one corner houses a branch of Artespaña, a state-run handicrafts shop.

If you are ready for lunch, go up Calle Reyes Católicos to the **Plaza Isabel la Católica**, dominated by a statue (pictured left) commemorating this queen's support for Columbus. From here you can take Calle Pavaneras to the small, tree-shaded, car-cluttered **Plaza Padre Suarez**, where **Seis Peniques** offers a range of set menus in an alfresco setting opposite the Casa de los Tiros, an early 16th century mansion – note the muskets peeping from the upper windows. For a classier venue with expensive but exquisite cuisine, try out the cellar-restaurant at the bottom of this plaza, **La Alacena** (Tel: 958 221 105).

Shopping

What to Buy

If the souvenir-sellers had their way we'd all return with suitcases full of gypsy costumes, personalised bullfighting posters, castanets, mantillas, Mezquita wine-flasks and Alhambra table-lamps. Don't let such mass-produced memories of Andalusia obscure the fact that specialist shops sell quality versions of these clichés: hats, fans, hand-made shawls, guitars and wrought ironwork (*esparto*).

Leather goods, jewellery and ceramics are widely sold – keep an eye out for shoes and sandals, silver filigree, decorative plates and bowls, *azulejos* and kitchenware – all particularly good value. In recent years the quality of handicraft products has improved, with good modern designs of hats, T-shirts, jewellery and stationery now available. Cheap belts, wallets, bags and baskets can be bought from African hawkers who will barter; look out too for the bargain shops specialising in goods sold for a few hundred pesetas.

If you're searching for locally made presents consider sherry, convent-made sweets, virgin olive oil, cassettes of guitar music, figs,

Flamenco dresses

honey, almonds and saffron. Other favourite Spanish purchases are *cava* (champagne – try the Delapierre or Freixenet labels), cigars from the Canary Islands or Cuba, carved olive wood utensils, terracotta kitchenware, *paella* dishes, candle-holders, *sangría* jugs, Lladró porcelain, *alfombras* (carpets and floor-rugs) and *jarapas* (multi-coloured rugs and car-seat covers made from cotton strips). Department stores provide essentials such as clothes and stationery.

Seville

Seville's main shopping street is the serpentine **Calle Sierpes**. This is the place to go for fashionable clothes as well as more "típico" fare, from fans to ceramics. Martian (No 48) offers a pleasing display of Sevillian ceramics and pottery. Zadi (No 48) has a serious collection of fans, mantillas and Lladró porcelain, while the old-fashioned Marquedano (No 40) stocks a classic range of Andalusian hats.

To the east, the Plaza de Jesús de la Pasión is the city's matrimony corner, with several jewellery shops. Beyond the northern end of Calle Sierpes you come to the Plaza del Duque de la Victoria, with Spain's largest department store, El Corte Inglés. Around the corner on Calle Alfonso XII, next to Marks & Spencers, Sevilla Rock sells Spanish pop and guitar music including flamenco and *sevillanas*.

Cerámica Santa Ana

For ceramics, La Alacena (further down Alfonso XII, at No 25) has top-of-the-range china and crockery from the famous British-owned La Cartuja factory (now located on the Carretera de Mérida). Puerta Triana (corner of Calle Santas Patronas and Calle Reyes Católicos) has a less expensive selection of painted plates, bowls and jugs while across the bridge in Triana, Cerámica Santa Ana (Calle San Jorge 31) is a rambling showroom-cum-pottery with enough antique and modern azulejos to turn your home into a mini-*alcázar*.

On the east side of the Maestranza bull-ring, Jamón Real I – Esther Fernández Fdez. (Calle López de Arenas 5) sells Extremaduran wines, meats and cheeses, including goat's cheese, marmalade and home-made wines and liqueurs. It also has a small bar where you can sample products, and there's another branch, Jamón Real II, at Calle Pastor y Landero 2.

Being a university town, Seville has some wonderful book shops. One of the best is Vértice, across from the Old Tobacco Factory on Calle San Fernando, which also has books in English.

Ceramics from Granada

Córdoba

Our word 'cordwainer' is derived from Córdoba and testifies to the city's long tradition of high quality leather-work. In the city bordering La Mezquita you'll not only find leather goods on sale in souvenir shops but also in small studios and cobblers' workshops like that at Calle Magistral González Francés 7 which specialises in riding boots. Silver filigree (*filigrana de plata*) is common. Look out also for two distinctive types of ceramic plate: the green and white Caliphal pottery based on 10th century Arab designs, and the heavy dark green pottery from nearby Lucena. Montilla wines and anisflavoured *licor* from Rute are other specialities.

In the small shops and stalls that surround the Plaza de la Corredera you'll find tyre-soled sandals, iron rings for hanging up flowerpots, barbecue utensils and wickerwork chairs, baskets, hampers and linen chests. Near the Ayuntamiento the *guarnicionería* Rafael Estevez Lopez (Calle San Pablo 6) sells saddles, riding tackle and woollen blankets while ACA Artesanía (Calle Torres Cabrera 9) is an outlet for handicrafts made by the Asociación Cordobesa de Artesanos. This sells well-designed leather duffle bags, wallets, stationery, silverplated jewellery, toys and ceramics.

Granada

Granada's souvenirs play heavily on the city's Moorish past – embossed leather, marquetry chessboards, inlaid furniture, and a distinctive blue and green pottery known as *Fajalauza* are the most obvious examples. The Albaicín is the best place to chance upon these but you'll also find them in the Cuesta de Gomérez at the foot of Alhambra hill. Woven products from the Alpujarras mountains are worth looking at – the Tejidos Fortuny workshop (Plaza de Fortuny 1) has some lively designs of rugs and wall-hangings.

Granada's main shopping precinct lies in the streets south and east of the cathedral. Calle Pescadería has small friendly shops selling meats and cheeses

Silkworms for sale in Seville's Alfalfa market

and a stall opposite the Bar Boca has good *Fajalauza* pottery. You may find interesting bargains in the Alcaicería (the old silk-market), but elsewhere it's wall-to-wall shoeshops. If you're only here for a short stay you'd be far better off spending your money on a box of mouth-exploding cakes from Flor y Nata (Calle Mesones 51) or Lopez Mezquita (Calle Reyes Católicos 29) and heading up to the Alhambra to scoff them in the sun.

Dyed chicks in Córdoba's Corredera market

Markets

Markets are the best place to buy fresh food from the surrounding countryside. Their stalls are a cornucopia of Andalusian produce: honey, goats' cheese, spiced meats and hams, snails, seafood, olives, nuts, bread and countless glorious fruits. Markets always start early in the morning and pack up around 1pm, apart from the weekend flea markets which often linger on until 3pm.

In **Seville** every district hosts its own daily fresh produce market – one of the most central is in the Plaza de la Encarnación and another is across the Triana bridge (turn right) on the site of the old Inquisition headquarters. A small weekday arts-and-crafts market loiters outside El Corte Inglés in the Plaza del Duque de la Victoria. In the north of the city there's a centuries-old flea market on Thursday in Calle Feria known as 'El Jueves'. Nearby in the Alameda de Hércules a similar bric-a-brac market takes place on Sunday mornings. At the same time there's a bird and pet market (including silkworms) in the Plaza de la Alfalfa, and an earnest stamp-and-coin collector's market in the Plaza del Cabildo.

In **Córdoba** the main market venue is the Corredera. In the week there's a covered *mercado* selling fresh produce while stalls outside sell fabric, clothes, plants and household items. On weekends this becomes a flea market. **Granada's** nicest market is in the Plaza Larga in the Albaicín, but you'll find a better range in the Mercado de San Agustín on the southwest corner of the cathedral.

Andalusian Cuisine

Seville claims to have invented *tapas* (snacks and appetizers) and can even tell you the bar where this national custom originated: El Rinconcillo (near the Santa Catalina church, Calle Gerona 40) where the staff developed the habit of covering a glass of *fino* with a *tapa* (lid) of ham. Today *tapas* are found everywhere and can be anything from a saucer of spiced olives or some slices of *jamón serrano* (mountain ham) to a gourmet nibble of oranges, onions and *bacalao* (dried cod), or a hot terracotta dish of *paella*.

A *tapa* or *porción* is simply a taster, while a *ración* is a small dish, often cooked. Lunch is the best time for *raciones* – the daily menu will be written on a board or the dishes just put out on the counter. Most bars serve *tapas* but only some treat it as an artform. Often the bill turns out to be as costly as a meal but the repeated frisson of *fino* and *gambas* (prawns), or *cerveza* and *boquerones* (anchovies in garlic and vinegar), is quintessential Spain. If you're a serious *tapas*-addict head straight for Seville to investigate Modesto (Calle Cano y Cueto 5) or the Hostelería del Laurel (Plaza de los Venerables) in the Barrio Santa Cruz and Casa Manolo (Calle San Jorge) in Triana.

Most bars have an alarming array of mountain hams and spiced

Tapas bar in Seville

sausages suspended from the ceiling, all tagged like prize antiques. You could also try some *salchichón* (salami), *chorizo* (red spicy sausage) or *morcilla* (blood sausage) while *habas con jamón* (broad beans with ham) is a typical Granada dish. *Gazpacho* is another famous Andalusian creation, a chilled soup based on bread and olive oil and flavoured with vegetables and herbs – usually tomatoes, garlic and peppers. The Córdobans make their own, thicker version called *salmorejo* while *ajo blanco* is a white soup from Málaga based on garlic, almonds and fruit.

In restaurants look for regional dishes signposted with words like *andaluz, a la granadina* or *alpujarreño* (from the Alpujarras mountains). Some chefs embrace Andalusia's Moorish heritage with dishes that combine the sweet and the savoury, perhaps by using honey, fruit or raisins to spice meat and poultry. Dishes cooked in sherry or incorporating almonds are common, as are country stews (*cocido* or the simpler *puchero*) which may mix chicken, ham, sausage and egg with *garbanzos* (chick-peas), rice or potatoes.

Despite fields full of vegetables, few seem to make it onto Spanish menus. Asparagus, artichokes, aubergines (*berenjenas*) and peppers do pop up but salad is a more common complement to a main dish. There is nearly always a *revuelto* (scrambled egg dish) on the menu, perhaps mixed with salmon, mushrooms, spinach or asparagus – useful if you are vegetarian. *Tortilla sacromonte* is a Granada dish where an omelette is invaded by ham, peas and assorted offal.

Having access to both the Atlantic and Mediterranean coasts Andalusia is blessed with fresh and plentiful fish and seafood. Tuna has been a staple ingredient since pre-Roman times and sardines, swordfish (*pez espada*) and skate (*raya*) frequently feature on menus. Cuts from large fish are often served with a saffron, paprika or tomato sauce while *zarzuela* is a fish stew with a spiced tomato sauce. Fried fish can be bought in take-away *freidurías*.

Desserts always include a choice of fresh fruit or ice cream but in better quality restaurants you'll be able to dither over *tarta de almendras* (almond tart), *crema de membrillo con queso* (quince jelly with cheese), *pastel cordobés* (puff pastry with candied fruit) or the *tocino de cielo* (caramel custard) from Cádiz.

In cities like Seville, Córdoba and Granada people never seem to stop eating. Mornings are when work gets done and breakfast is but a meditative moment. Anything goes as long as it's quick: coffee and brandy, chocolate and *churros* (extrusions of sweet battered dough), bread dunked in olive oil, toast and dripping – all taken standing at the bar in a humble pose no doubt learned at confession. By 11am the mood shifts cakewards or to an elevenses ice-cream, but by noon the emphasis changes again as the bar staff start putting out their freshly-made *tapas*.

By 7pm it's time for the *paseo* and an obligatory ice cream, after which the *tapas* appear again around 8pm. Restaurants are in action by 9pm but rarely full before 10pm – at weekends they will still be serving new customers at midnight. After which the night is young; a good time to drink an *oloroso*, toy with a sticky cake, think what you'll have for breakfast....

Specific restaurant recommendations are included in the individual city itineraries earlier in this book. Ignore the 'fork' rating system and don't expect price to be a guarantee of quality – remember

Heavenly sweets (see opposite)

too that it is quite acceptable to just order a starter or one course if that's all you want. Keep some cash in reserve as not all restaurants take credit cards. Don't ask for the *menú del día* (menu of the day) when you really mean the *especialidad del día* (speciality of the day) – the first is a basic, low price set-meal all restaurants must offer by law (usually only advertised outside by price and often quite boring), the latter is whatever's fresh and in season.

Drinks

Andalusia's most famous drink is sherry, a fortified wine from Jerez de la Frontera. We are familiar with it as an aperitif but the Spanish will drink it with a meal and indeed whenever they can find an excuse. It is the classic complement to *tapas*.

Fino is the most common drink – a light, dry sherry, always served chilled. *Amontillado* is mellower with a nutty flavour and an amber hue. *Oloroso* is mature, dark and rich, often drunk as a dessert wine. *Palo cortado* is richer than *amontillado* but lighter than *oloroso*. You should also try

Sherry is perfect with tapas

manzanilla, a *fino* made in Sanlúcar de Barrameda on the Atlantic coast where the salty sea air gives it a distinctive tang.

Andalusian wines are few and come a poor second to their sherries. Exceptions are the excellent strong white Montilla-Moriles, produced in Córdoba (*amontillado* means 'like a Montilla'), and the sweet dessert wines made in Málaga from muscatel grapes.

Brandies are also produced around Jerez, varying from the cheap, highly addictive Soberano to the luxurious Carlos I. You may wish to suffer Andalusia's assorted firewaters too: the intrepid will discover a bewildering range of local *aguardientes*, variously flavoured with almonds, cherries, oranges, apricots and anis. Spanish measures of spirits are liberal, so take care.

The predominant beer is made by Cruzcampo – *una caña* is normally taken to mean a small glass of draught, *una cerveza* a large glass or a bottle. *Horchata* is an almond milk while *zumos* are heavenly fruit juices freshly-squeezed before your eyes – try a mix of *naranja* (orange) and *limón* (lemon). Bottled water is either *agua con gas* (with bubbles) or *sin gas*. Ice is unlikely to be from bottled water so if you want to avoid it ask for your drink *sin hielo*. Black coffee is *café solo*, white *con leche* and *cortado* somewhere in between. And cheers is *salud*!

Heavenly Sweets

Sweets, pastries, cakes and biscuits have been made in Andalusia's convents since the Reconquest, a sweet-toothed tradition inherited from the Arabs. Today they can still be bought from the nuns themselves. The recipe for *yemas* is centuries old, originally made from the surplus egg yolks donated to the convents after the whites had been used to clarify the wines of Jerez and Montilla. Those sold in Seville's San Leandro convent are the most famous (see Itinerary 3) but every convent makes its own delicacies.

Biscuits flavoured with honey, cinnamon, sesame, ginger or almonds are less sugary – try some *alfajores* or *polvorones* made by the Convento de Santa Isabel de los Angeles in Córdoba (near the Palacio de Viana). For a comprehensive selection of sweets from Seville's many convent-confectioneries visit El Torno (see Itinerary 2).

Bullfights

Bullfights (*corridas*) are frequently shown on Spanish television, and for many people that's quite enough. If you're keen to attend in person Seville's La Maestranza is one of the top rings in Spain. Córdoba boasts Las Califas, one of the largest *plaza de toros* in the country (on the western edge of the city) and there's also a bull-ring in Granada off the Avenida de Madrid (tickets sold at Calle Escudo del Carmen 18).

In Andalusia the bullfighting season opens with the daily *corridas* held at Seville's Feria, and these are often some of the best fights of the year. *Corridas* continue in the city throughout May, held every Sunday at 6 or 7pm. By then the major stars will be appearing at the May Fairs held in Córdoba, Jerez de la Frontera (where the bulls are still fought on horseback), Ecija, Granada and numerous other towns. Through the summer months *corridas* only take place as a part of a local fiesta with the regular programme resumed during September and October. Posters advertising the fights are widely displayed.

Tickets for the top *corridas* can be expensive and hard to get. If you're prepared to pay for a quality spectacle it will be more apparent why bullfighting is considered an art rather than a sport. The best place to buy tickets is direct from the *Despacho Oficial de Localidades* at the *plaza de toros* but you'll also find that kiosks appear in city-centre doorways on the day before a *corrida*. These may charge a commission. Seats in the shade (*sombra*) are more expensive than those in the sun (*sol*), and you also normally pay more for a seat near the ringside (*barrera*). Fights that include young bulls (*novillos*) usually take place at the end of the season and are cheaper.

A *corrida* is a series of six fights in which three matadors each dispatch two bulls. Each fight is a three-act drama accompanied by the tragicomic comments of a brass band. First the *bravo toro* enters and is teased and assessed by the matador and his *cuadrilla*

(team); the matador then confronts the bull alone, using his cape to mock and enrage the beast. Next a *picador* enters mounted on horseback (it is only in this century that the horses were given protective padding), who uses a lance to damage the bull's neck muscles. The acrobatic *banderilleros* follow, who drive colourful darts into this wound. Next the matador takes his red cloth and leads the weakened animal in a merry dance of death with slow, deft passes that reveal the extent of his courage and skill. Finally the matador thrusts his sword into the bull's heart – if it is a clean death and the matador has performed with exceptional style handkerchiefs will be waved by the crowd and, in outstanding cases, the matador will be awarded one or even two of the bull's ears.

Flamenco

Flamenco's origins are mysterious – quite appropriate for a dance form that demands spontaneity, deep emotion and an elusive, quasi-demonic power to enchant known as *duende*. Elements of ancient Indian, Arab and Jewish music have been detected in its sorrowful and discordant songs and dances, although the present guitar-backed form only evolved in the mid-18th century. Flamenco was the creation of Andalusia's gypsy communities, particularly those that settled in the Atlantic-facing lands between Seville and Cádiz. As these *gitanos* sought work throughout the rest of Spain new local styles developed: by the late 19th century flamenco had shed its peasant

Flamenco's origins are mysterious

image and become a public property with its own established rules and repertoire.

Today flamenco is crossing over into jazz and rock, and still evolving. For many it is the essence of Spain, the soul of Andalusia; for others it is just a painful caterwauling. Because it is by nature impulsive and improvised flamenco cannot lend itself to repeated public performance. Every city has its flamenco tourist shows, variously described as *tablaos* or *zambras*, which attract the vitriol of purists. They perform the fast, light-hearted *cante chico* rather than the slow, knife-in-the-heart *cante jondo*. That said, don't be put off attending a *tablao* because it's not the real McCoy. Most hotels sell tickets, inclusive of transport and a drink.

In **Seville** try Los Gallos (Plaza Santa Cruz 11) in the Barrio Santa Cruz – probably the oldest and most successful *tablao* in Andalusia, or the less tourist-wooing Tablao de Curro Vélez (Calle Rodó 7) near the bullring. In **Granada** head for the gypsy caves of Sacromonte. Unfortunately the locals seem to send out their creepiest guys to tout for business which can be off-putting – Cuevas del Rocío (Camino del Sacromonte) is the best of a mixed bunch.

For 'authentic' flamenco (which to the uninitiated may not appear all that different), music festivals, flamenco competitions and the performances staged at fiestas offer good opportunities. Seville's Feria, Córdoba's triennial Flamenco Festival and Granada's International Music and Dance Festival are three of the best.

Typical tablao in action

Nightlife

For many Spaniards nightlife simply means *paseo* and *tapeo*. Promenading by the river in the evening sun or taking a gossipy walk down a central shopping street – followed by some serious *tapas* bar-hopping and/or a meal in a restaurant – is quite enough for a good night out. For wilder action in **Seville** head for the Barrio Santa Cruz or Triana (the streets west of Calle Betis); the free 'what's on' magazine *El Giraldillo* has up-to-date listings. Discotheques tend to dance in waves with teenagers arriving around

74

Cheers from the local brewery

11pm and an older clientele following on about 1am: the enormous RRRrio (Calle Betis, closed Monday) caters for young lunatics and El Coto below the Hotel Los Lebreros (Calle Luis de Morales 2) for older ones.

In **Granada** the streets around the University (Calle Pedro Antonio de Alarcón) set the party pace which in term-time can spread to the Sacromonte caves. For discos try the large Granada 10 (Calle Cárcel Baja 38) or Queen's Disco (Calle Arabial); Perkusion (Plaza de García) attracts teenagers.

Theatres and Concert Halls

Seville
TEATRO DE LA MAESTRANZA,
Paseo Colón. Tel: 95 422 3344
TEATRO LOPE DE VEGA, *Avenida María Luisa.Tel: 95 459 0853*

Córdoba
GRAN TEATRO, *Avenida Gran Capitán. Tel: 957 48 02 37*

Granada
TEATRO ISABEL LA CATOLICA, *Acera del Darro. Tel: 958 22 02 69*
AUDITORIO MANUEL DE FALLA, *Paseo de los Mártires. Tel: 958 22 21 88*

Sport

Seville has two **football** teams, Sevilla (Estadio Sánchez Pizjuán in the east of the city) and Real Betis (Estadio Benito Villamarín in the south). Matches are normally played at 5pm on Sunday – any local paper or Sevillian should be able to tell you when the next fixture is.

The best **golf** courses in the region are actually on the Costa del Sol, where they are as much of an attraction as the beaches, but close to Seville is the 18-hole Real Club de Golf de Sevilla (Tel 95 412 4301). In Córdoba Los Villares (Tel: 957 35 02 08) has 18 holes, as does Granada's Club de Golf (Tel: 958 58 44 36).

For information on **skiing** you should contact the Sierra Nevada Ski Resort (Tel: 958 24 91 11).

For information on **hiking**, **riding**, **mountain biking**, **hang-gliding** and other adventurous pursuits in the Sierra Nevada and Alpujarras contact Nevadensis (Tel: 958 76 31 27).

Calendar of Special Events

The Andalusians joke that every day, somewhere in the region, there's a fiesta going on. When you add in the boisterous stream of cultural events that major cities like Seville, Córdoba and Granada stage through the year it is inevitable that your visit will co-incide with some religious holiday, local fair or arts festival.

The most spectacular and engrossing events take place between March and June. Seville's famous, histrionic **Semana Santa** (Holy Week) processions top the bill followed closely by the city's extravagant **Feria** (April Fair). Both celebrations attract large numbers of people and accommodation consequently becomes scarce and expensive – book well ahead. In May, Córdoba's **Patio Festival** and **Feria** continue the party mood while Granada's main celebrations take place around **Corpus Christi**.

To find out what's on look out for the colourful posters that warn of approaching fiestas or ask in a hotel or Tourist Office. The following calendar is only a guide and you should check dates before setting out – in Spain everything is a moveable fiesta.

JANUARY

The old year is normally seen off with a cacophony of fireworks and car horns. Tradition says you should swallow a grape (and a sip of *cava* if you're quick) for each strike of the midnight clock. Needless to say **Año Nuevo** (New Year's Day) is a public holiday.

On the second Granada celebrates the victory of the Catholic Monarchs over the city's Moorish rulers in 1492 with the **Día de la Toma** (Day of the Capture). Regal treasures bequeathed

SEVILLA
FIESTAS DE PRIMAVERA·1930·SEMANA SANTA
FERIA EN EL RECINTO DE LA
EXPOSICION IBERO_AMERICANA

Poster for the spring fiestas

by Ferdinand and Isabella are carried through the city and commemorative events held in the Cathedral and Capilla Real.

On the fifth the **Cabalgata del los Reyes Magos** (Calvacade of the Three Kings) celebrates their arrival with a colourful procession. The following day (the sixth) is a public holiday marking **Epiphany** (Twelfth Night), the day when Spanish children finally get their Christmas presents.

FEBRUARY

On the first Granada holds a local fiesta in honour of its patron saint **San Cecilio**, including a pilgrimage to the Sacromonte catacombs. At the end of the month, **Andalusia Day** (27–28th) is a public holiday and celebration throughout the region.

Since the death of Franco, February in Spain has also meant **Carnaval**, an exuberant excuse for spectacular floats, fireworks, dancing and irreverence to spread to towns and villages throughout the land.

During February or March Seville stages its annual **Festival of Ancient Music** featuring early works played on authentic instruments.

MARCH/APRIL

Semana Santa (Holy Week) is a serious religious celebration with everything closed on Holy Thursday and Good Friday. Holy Week inspires the most fervent religious celebrations in the Andalusian calendar. Those held in Seville are renowned for the intense dramatic spectacle they create, but you'll find Semana Santa observed with similar panache in Málaga and with equal solemnity in Córdoba and Granada.

Events commence on Palm Sunday when religious and social organisa-

tions known as *cofradías* (brotherhoods) start carrying revered statues and images from their chapels towards the city cathedral. Enormous ornately-decorated floats known as *pasos* are used to transport these figureheads. These precious, cumbersome platforms are steered through the narrow streets, urged on by drum bands and lamenting crowds with some individuals bursting into *saetas* – brief, anguished hymns. Behind the *pasos* march columns of *nazarenos*, penitents wearing conical hoods and carrying long lighted candles.

In Seville over 100 such processions take place in the course of the week. In order to witness the greatest of these emotional tableaux – for example those involving El Gran Poder, La Esper-

Feria procession

anza de Triana and La Macarena which pass through the city in the early hours of Good Friday – consult timetables and official routes published in daily newspapers like *ABC*, or seek the advice of a Sevillian.

Surprisingly Granada also stages an **International Tango Festival** in the first week of March. The 19th of March is **San José** (St Joseph's Day), a public holiday in some towns.

In mid-April Seville ignites again with its **Feria** (April Fair), a week-long fiesta of drinking, dancing and bullfighting with horse parades and Andalusian pageantry. The Feria de Abril began life in the 1850s as a horse fair and agricultural market but gradually developed to become the best-known secular party in Andalusia.

Every spring a vast area of the Los Remedios district is transformed into a gaudy kaleidoscope of fairground attractions bordered by rows of striped drinking tents known as *casetas*. A week of sophisticated hedonism ensues with most participants dressed for the occasion – *señoritas* in bright flamenco costume cling to horsemen in wide-brimmed hats, Sevillian ladies bedecked with flowers and mantillas parade in carriages.

The day begins at noon with parades and itinerant exhibitionism, followed by bullfights at La Maestranza in the early evening. At night there is the fairground and flamenco, more *fino* and *tapas*, and ceaseless conversation. It is one of Spain's great exuberant festivals, a potent mix of corporate hospitality and gypsy singers, of banquets given by wealthy Sevillian families and shindigs hosted by political parties and trade unions. It is said that as much sherry is drunk in Feria week as is normally consumed in Spain during a year.

MAY/JUNE

On the first the **Día del Trabajo** (Labour Day) is suitably marked by a day off work. The opening days of the month are also when the *Cruces de Mayo* (Crosses of May) appear in many towns, crosses elaborately decorated with flowers that are set up in the street to herald the arrival of spring. They are best seen in Granada (especially in the Albaicín) or in Córdoba, and form the focus for a fiesta

usually held on the third. This first week is normally when the sherry capital Jerez de la Frontera holds its annual Horse Fair.

After the extravagances of Seville, May is the month when Córdoba comes alive – beginning with its charming **Festival de los Patios** (Patio Festival) usually held in the first fortnight. This is when the Córdobans open up their flower-filled courtyards to all-comers, with concerts and flamenco performances held in the neighbouring plazas.

The city's festive mood culminates in the May **Feria**, held at the end of the month, when the streets are graced by elegant horse-riders dressed in Andalusian costume and the parks are packed with stalls and marquees. Every three years the city also finds the energy to stage a **National Flamenco Competition**.

Not to be outdone Granada holds an **International Drama Festival** in early May while Seville stages a cultural programme of fringe theatre, dance, exhibitions and music known as 'Cita en Sevilla' (April–June). On the 30th there is a local fiesta in Seville in honour of San Fernando. At Pentecost (Whitsun) at least half a million pilgrims descend on **El Rocío**, an isolated village to the north of Las Marismas, the marshland that lies at the mouth of the Guadalquivir river. It is the biggest *romería* (country festival) in Spain.

Corpus Christi (late May or early June) is another important Catholic celebration and public holiday honoured throughout Spain. In Seville and Córdoba choirboys in medieval dress known as Los Seises perform set dances before the Cathedral altar, while in Granada the occasion inspires the city's principal fiesta with processions and bullfights, as well as flamenco competitions and a fair.

Cruces de Mayo celebration

Performance art festival poster

JUNE/JULY

From mid-June to mid-July Granada stages its acclaimed **International Festival of Music and Dance** which attracts top stars from the world of classical music, jazz and ballet. Some concerts take place in Charles V's palace and the patios of the Alhambra, with dance performances in the gardens of the Generalife.

Córdoba holds a prestigious **International Guitar Festival** in the first half of July with classical, flamenco and Latin music. In Seville there is an **International Festival of Theatre and Dance**.

AUGUST

On the 15th there is a public holiday for **Asunción** (Assumption), and in Seville a local fiesta, the **Feast of the Virgen de los Reyes**. During the last week the Río Guadalquivir is honoured with a festival in the sherry town of Sanlúcar de Barrameda – events include flamenco competitions and horse-racing along the beach.

SEPTEMBER

The first two weeks of September finds Ronda holding its **Feria** and *corrida goyesca*, a fight staged with participants wearing 18th-century costume in honour of Pedro Romero. On the eighth, Córdoba celebrates its patron saint, the **Virgen de la Fuensanta**. On the last Sunday there is a fiesta in Granada in honour of the city's patroness **Nuestra Señora las Angustias**, while on the 29th in the Albaicín **San Miguel** is honoured with a fiesta and procession up to the hermitage San Miguel el Alto.

Every two years (even-numbered years) Seville stages a **Festival of Flamenco** at the end of the month.

OCTOBER

Christopher Columbus's 'discovery' of America is celebrated on the 12th with a public holiday, **Día de la Hispanidad**. There is also a local fiesta on the 24th in Córdoba in honour of **San Rafael**.

NOVEMBER

On the first of the month, **Todos los Santos** (All Saints' Day) is a public holiday. The cities of Seville and Granada stage **International Jazz Festivals** in November.

DECEMBER

Constitution Day on the sixth is a public holiday, followed by another on the eighth, **Inmaculada Concepción** (the Immaculate Conception). **Navidad** (Christmas) is a time for parties, which go on in earnest for the full twelve days of the season.

On the 28th Spaniards celebrate their equivalent of April Fool's Day, **Día de los Inocentes** (Day of the Holy Innocents).

Practical Information

hambra consequently one of the most delightful places you could spend a Spanish summer.

TRAVEL ESSENTIALS

When to Go

Spring is the best time to visit Andalusia: any week from early March, when the orange trees are coming into blossom, to late May, when the fields and roadsides are awash with colourful wildflowers. This is the fiesta season too, when every town and village decorates its streets with flowers and coloured lights.

Accommodation for Seville's Semana Santa sells out a year in advance despite the fact that the price of a room is around treble what it is for the rest of the year.

For a quieter break try and slip into a week either side of these festivities, or come in autumn – ideally September or October. During the summer the Guadalquivir valley roasts – Ecija, almost mid-way between Seville and Córdoba, is known as *la sartén* (the frying-pan) of Spain – but don't be put off: Andalusian cities, with their narrow streets, patios and gardens are designed for this heat. Granada, with the advantage of being 2,247ft (685m) above sea level, is cooler and the Al-

Climate

In Seville and Córdoba winters are mild (12°C, 53°F) with the spring months serving as a delicious bridge into intensely hot summers that soar above 38°C (100°F) in June and July; autumn is a slow cooling-off period as the baked land recovers. In Granada these transitions are more abrupt – spring and autumn are short, summers hot and dry (25°C, 77°F) and winters cold (6°C, 43°F). Rain tends to fall between October and March, often in sudden heavy downpours, but for most of the year the sun shines.

Time Difference

Along with the rest of Europe, Spain is one hour ahead of Britain. Spanish Summer Time runs from the last Sunday in March to the last Sunday in October.

Documents

All visitors require a valid passport or a national identity card (if a citizen of an EU country). Visitors from outside the EU, US, Australia and New Zealand must obtain a visa before entering Spain. Motorists will need an international driving permit (available from international motoring organisations) or EU format three-part driving licence, along with adequate insurance.

Money Matters

Traveller's cheques, Eurocheques and credit cards are all accepted, though far from universally. Many hotels will not accept personal cheques and not all restaurants or shops take credit cards; a cashpoint card is useful. Get some pesetas before you go.

Health

No vaccinations are required but health insurance is recommended. Form E111 entitles EU nationals to reciprocal medical benefits. A strong sun cream is essential.

Clothing

Seville, Córdoba and Granada are all smart, fashionable cities and their citizens enjoy wearing good clothes. In the summer you'll need sunglasses, sunhat and swimming costume, but also something warm for the evenings and air-conditioned buildings; in winter a jumper and anorak will be necessary. Wear comfortable shoes at all times. A money-belt is a good idea.

Electricity

220 Volts. Sockets take round two-point plugs (European size). Most UK appliances will need an adaptor.

Photography

Film is relatively expensive in Spain and some types are not always avail-

able – develop it when you get home. Carry spare camera batteries.

On Departure

In recent years Spain has had its share of air traffic delays so always confirm your return flight.

GETTING THERE

By Air

Iberia operates scheduled flights from London to Seville, Jerez de la Frontera, Málaga and Granada – some flights involve a stop-over at Madrid or Barcelona (Tel: 020-7830 0011) in the UK. Other scheduled carriers operate into Málaga, Jerez de la Frontera and Gibraltar. Charter companies also offer good value flight-only deals to Málaga, Gibraltar and Faro in the Portuguese Algarve – look in the classified section of local and national newspapers.

Seville airport (San Pablo) is 7.5 miles (12km) east of the centre. There is a regular bus connection (30–40 minute trip) into the city or take a taxi for around 2,000 pesetas. For Airport Information tel: 95 444 90 00; Iberia Information, tel: 95 451 06 77.

Granada and Córdoba airports are served by domestic flights. Granada airport, tel: 958 24 52 00; Córdoba airport, tel: 957 21 41 00.

Package Deals

Travel companies offer tailor-made holidays visiting Seville, Córdoba and Granada. These include flight, accommodation and car hire. Seville is featured by several city-break specialists.

By Rail

National rail networks offer through-fare deals to Andalusia in the UK, contact Rail Europe, tel: 08705 848848. A high speed rail link has reduced the journey-time between Madrid and Seville to 2¾ hours. If you are travelling extensively in Spain consider buying an Inter-Rail card or the Tarjeta Turistica issued by the national rail network, RENFE.

Rail travellers can also tour Andalusia in elegant 1920s style by taking the luxurious Al-Andalus Express (bookable in the UK through Mundi Color, tel: 020-7828 6021).

By Road

British coach operators offer services to Spain by road to Seville, details from Eurolines UK(tel: 01582-404511). If you plan to take your own car consider cutting down on the driving by using the French Motorail link between Calais and Nice, contact Rail Europe, (tel: 08705-848848), or sailing from Plymouth to Santander with Brittany Ferries, (tel: 0990-360360).

GETTING AROUND

Seville is ideal for a short break and the best place in Andalusia for street-life, shopping and *tapas* bar-hopping. Córdoba is easily reached from Seville by rail or road and the two cities form a natural pair. Granada and the snow-capped Sierra Nevada are a refreshing contrast to the hot plains of the Guadalquivir valley.

Maps and Guides

The map accompanying this guide contains town plans of all three cities plus a regional map. If you are touring by car and require a larger area than the regional map shows, Michelin map No 446 *Andalusia and the Costa del Sol* is a good choice.

By Car

Drive on the right. Seat belts are compulsory outside built-up areas and motoring offences earn on-the-spot fines. In rural areas petrol stations may close on Sundays or for a siesta; most, but not all, take credit cards.

If you take back roads in the countryside you'll have a longer journey but a far more rewarding trip. In the cities you'll just have to take a road that isn't blocked or dug up. The Spanish treat inner-city driving as if it was a motorised bullfight, which means they see it as an art-form and therefore something to be enjoyed.

Car Hire

Compared with most other European countries car hire in Spain is inexpensive. Many airlines and package companies offer good value fly-drive deals, and if you know your requirements it's simplest to book before you arrive.

It's also easy to hire cars in Spain, although some firms will not rent to drivers under 21 or with less than a year's experience. In any case, hire companies will need to see your passport and international driving licence or national driving licence. It is sensible to pay a little extra for Collision Damage Waiver and Personal Accident insurance in addition to the statutory Third Party insurance.

Motorbikes and mopeds offer another way of getting around and are easily rented – the age limits are 18 and 16 respectively.

By Train

There are frequent trains between Seville and Córdoba. Connections from either of these cities to Granada or Málaga (3–5 hours) go via the notorious Bobadilla Junction and normally involve a change of train. The journey up from Málaga to Bobadilla is spectacular.

The Spanish have an alarming number of train classifications. Speediest are the sleek *Talgos* (supplements and reservation required), followed by the *Expresos* and *Rápidos* (both quite straightforward trains); then there are the lazy *Directos* and *Interurbanos*, followed by the utterly slothful *Tranvías*. For a timetable ask for an *horario de trenes*.

RENFE Information:
Seville Tel: 95 454 0202
Córdoba Tel: 957 49 02 02
Granada Tel: 958 27 12 72

By Coach and Bus

Between Seville and Córdoba there's little to choose between train or coach but for the longer journey to or from Granada the coach is more direct and arguably more scenic. Always take a coach if you are travelling between Málaga and Granada. The most useful company is Alsina Graells who operate an express service between Seville and Córdoba as well as other routes from these cities to Granada and Málaga (tel: Seville 95 441 8811; Córdoba 957 23 64 74; Granada 958 18 54 80).

If you are doing a lot of trips in Seville buy a *bonobus* 10-journey ticket or a *tarjeta turistica* (tourist pass) valid for 3 or 7 days. To visit the Itálica ruins take a bus to Santiponce.

In Córdoba the main bus station is at Avenida de Medina Azahara 29. In Granada the main station is on the Carretera de Jaén.

By Taxi

Taxis are a cheap, reliable and readily available way of getting around these three cities. A green *libre* sign indicates that a taxi is for hire. Agree a price first for long journeys or tours.

Taxi Numbers
Seville Tel: 95 458 00 00/462 22 22.
Córdoba Tel: 957 47 02 91.
Granada Tel: 958 28 06 54.

ACCOMMODATION

Hotels

The best hotels fill up quickly. If you're taking a short break you may prefer to book an all-inclusive flight and accommodation package before you leave, plus car hire if you require it. If you are touring, ring ahead to book a room – the hotel will probably ask you to arrive by a certain time, so ring again to let them know if you will be late. Some hotels, such as the Paradors or those close to the Alhambra, are best booked as soon as you know the required dates. Hotels range from 1–5 star. Approximate prices for a double room with bath are:

★★★★★	20,000–40,000 pesetas
★★★★	15,000–30,000 pesetas
★★★	10,000–20,000 pesetas
★★	5,000–10,000 pesetas
★	5,000–8,000 pesetas

IVA (Spanish VAT) of 7 percent is added to all hotel bills. You may also encounter Hotel Residencias (HR) which only serve breakfast and Apartment Hotels where rooms have kitchen facilities. *Hostales*, graded 1–3 star, are small family-run hotels offering simple accommodation that varies from the brilliant to the dismal – always see the room before you accept. Other variations are the *Pensión* (P), *Fonda* (F) and *Casas de Huéspedes* (CH). Self-cat-

ering apartments (*apartamentos turisticos*) are best booked through an agent. The minimum stay is normally a week.

A detailed list of hotels in each of these cities is available from the Spanish Tourist Office in London. Paradors (state-run luxury hotels) can be booked in the UK through Keytel International (tel: 0171-402 8182).

Seville

There is no Parador in Seville – the nearest is in Carmona, the **PARADOR DE TURISMO ALCAZAR DEL REY DON PEDRO**★★★★ (tel: 95 414 10 10). Other possibilities in the luxury bracket include: the wonderfully grand 1920s **ALFONSO XIII**★★★★★ (Calle San Fernando 2, tel: 95 422 28 50), the **DOÑA MARIA**★★★★ (in Calle Don Remondo 19, tel: 95 422 49 90) and the **HOTEL MACARENA**★★★★ (Calle San Juan de Ribera 2, tel: 95 437 58 00).

Both the **HOTEL LA RABIDA**★★ (Calle Castelar 24, tel: 95 422 09 60) and the **HOTEL SIMON**★ (Calle García de Vinuesa, tel: 95 422 66 00) are old patio-style hotels located close to the bull-ring while the pleasant **HOTEL MURILLO**★★ (Calle Lope de Rueda 7, tel: 95 421 60 95) is in the Barrio Santa Cruz.

Alfonso XIII hotel, Seville

Pension in Córdoba
Córdoba

The modern **PARADOR NACIONAL LA ARRAZUFA**★★★★ stands aloof on the edge of town (Avenida de La Arrazufa 33, tel: 957 27 59 00). Around the Mezquita the **HOTEL CONQUISTADOR**★★★ (Calle Magistral González Francés 15, tel: 957 48 11 02) and the **HOTEL MAIMONIDES**★★★ (Calle Torrijos 4, tel: 957 47 15 00) top the bill while the **HOTEL ALBUCASIS**★★ (Calle Buen Pastor 11, tel: 957 47 86 25) and **HOTEL MARISA**★★ (Calle Cardenal Herrero 6, tel: 957 47 31 42) are good alternatives. The **HOSTAL MAESTRE**★★ (Calle Romero Barros 16, tel: 957 47 53 95) and the **PENSION SÉNECA** (Calle Conde y Luque 7, tel: 957 47 32 34) are small, very friendly family affairs with typical patios.

Granada

The **PARADOR NACIONAL SAN FRANCISCO**★★★★ (Alhambra, tel: 958 22 14 40) inhabits a restored convent within the palace grounds – highly desirable but ring them now. The small **HOSTAL AMÉRICA**★ (closed November–February; Calle Real de la Alhambra 53, tel: 958 22 74 71) enjoys this privileged location too. Also on the Alhambra hill are the splendid neo-Moorish **HOTEL ALHAMBRA PALACE**★★★★ (Calle Peña Partida 2, tel: 958 22 14 68), the modern **HOTEL LOS ALIXARES**★★★ (Avenida Alixares del Generalife, tel: 958 22 55 75) and the good-value **PENSION DOÑA LUPE**★ (Avenida de los Alixares, tel: 958 22 14 73).

Down in the city centre the modern HOTEL MELIA GRANADA✩✩✩✩ is well-located on Calle Angel Ganivet 7 (tel: 958 22 74 00), while the large HOTEL LOS ANGELES (Cuesta Escoriaza 17, tel: 958 22 14 24) lies south of Campo del Príncipe.

Camping

Seville: Camping Sevilla, Carretera N-IV Madrid-Cádiz km534, tel: 95 451 43 79. 4 miles (6.4km) from city centre, open all year.

Córdoba: Campamento Municipal, Avenida de Brillante 50, Tel: 957 282 21 65. 3 miles (1.8km) from city centre, open all year.

Granada: Camping Sierra Nevada, Avenida de Madrid 107, Tel: 958 15 00 62. Open March–October.

USEFUL INFORMATION

Tourist Offices

Tourist offices in Spain are generally helpful but always busy – have a list of questions ready. All can give you free maps and information and those run by the Junta de Andalusia (listed first below) also have leaflets. Every large city has a Municipal Tourist Office as well (listed second) which primarily dispenses local information. Offices are normally open 9am–7pm Monday to Saturday and 10am–2pm on Sunday.
Seville Av de la Constitución 21, tel: 95 422 14 04; Costurero de la Reina, Paseo de la Delicias, tel: 95 423 44 65.
Córdoba Calle Torrijos 10 (Palacio de Congresos), tel: 957 47 12 35.
Granada Plaza Mariana Pineda 10, tel: 958 22 35 28; Corral del Carbón, tel. 958 22 59 90.
    In **London** the Spanish National Tourist Office is situated at 56 St James's Street, London SW1A 1LD, tel: 020-7486 8077, fax: 020-7629 4257.

Tipping and Service

Tipping is normal but not obligatory – 10 per cent for taxi-drivers and restaurants, at least 100 pesetas for hotel staff and waiters. Some restaurants will add a service charge but many people still leave a tip. In bars it costs more if you sit down at a table and are served by a waiter.

Facilities for the Disabled

Andalusia is a viable destination for disabled travellers, but facilities vary considerably. The best are found in the resorts of the Costa del Sol, although the HOTEL INGLATERRA✩✩✩✩ in Seville (tel: 95 422 49 70) is listed as having facilities for disabled guests. For more information consult a detailed guide such as the Royal Association for Disability and Rehabilitation's annual handbook *Holidays and Travel Abroad* available in libraries or from RADAR, 12 City Forum, 250 City Road, London EC1V 8AF. Tel: 020-7250 3222, fax: 020-7250 0212.

Children

The Spanish think that children should be seen, heard and utterly spoilt. They're not just tolerated but enjoyed, welcome guests in bars and restaurants. Most hotels can provide cots and highchairs (book ahead) while baby food, nappies, powdered milk and other necessities are available in supermarkets. Babysitters can be arranged through hotels or ask Tourist Offices about private services. Hire car firms can supply child seats but order in advance and take a sun-screen for the windows. It is against the law for children under 12 to travel in front seats. On RENFE children under four travel free, under 12 half-price.

Customs

There are no restrictions on the import of currencies. You can bring in personal belongings and souvenirs, as well as food for your own consumption. There are no restrictions on quantities of goods that can be imported/exported from other EU countries, as long as they are for personal use only. In July 1999, duty-free sales were abolished between EU countries. Visitors arriving from outside the EU can import (duty-free) 200 cigarettes, 50 cigars or 250g tobacco; 2 litres of wine, or 1 litre of spirits; 500g of coffee beans; 50g of perfume and 0.25 litres of toilet water. Tobacco and alcohol allowances are only for travellers aged 17 and over.

Consulates in Seville

Austria
Marqués de Paradas 26
Tel: 95 422 21 62.

United Kingdom
Plaza Nueva 8
Tel: 95 422 88 75.

France
Plaza de Santa Cruz 1
Tel: 95 422 28 96.

Germany
Avda. de la Palmera 19
Tel: 954 23 04 90.

Netherlands
Gravina 55
Tel: 95 422 87 50.

USA
Paseo de la Delicias 7.
Tel: 95 423 18 85.

MEDIA & COMMUNICATION

In Seville newspapers like *El Correo* and *Diario 16* publish listings of forthcoming cultural events in the city. In addition, a what's on magazine entitled *El Giraldillo* is published weekly and available free from Tourist Offices, museums and cultural venues. In Córdoba the daily paper *Córdoba* has a section of useful information including late-night chemists and train and bus timetables, as does *Ideal* in Granada.

Streetside newstand

Telephone

Phone boxes take most coins and you need to insert a minimum of 25 pesetas for a local call. Some now take phone cards (*tarjetas telefónicas*) which can be bought from news and tobacco kiosks. Calls can also be made from multi-boothed *cabinas* (kiosks) in the city centre where you pay an assistant afterwards. These are particularly useful for long-distance calls.

Main Telephone Offices:
Seville: Plaza Nueva 3.
Córdoba: Plaza de las Tendillas.
Granada: Calle Reyes Católicos.
    To call other countries, dial the international access code 00, then the country code: Australia (61); France (33); Germany (49); Italy (39); Japan (81); Netherlands (31); UK (44); US and Canada (1). Calls are cheaper between 10pm and 8am.

Phone Access Codes

Direct Enquiries 1003
British Telecom 900 990 044
ATT 900 990 011
MCI 900 990 014
Sprint 900 990 013

BUSINESS HOURS

Spanish hours are vulnerable to what happened the night before, but you will find the majority of businesses in action by around 9am. Activity then stops at 1 or 1.30pm – for the Spanish day is traditionally divided by a long lunch followed by a siesta, a practice well worth observing, especially in summer. Business resumes again about 4.30pm (5pm in summer) and continues until about 7 or 8pm. Government offices often start at 8am and work through until 3pm.

Banks are more punctual, and open 8.30am–2pm Monday to Friday. They are also open for business on Saturdays 8.30am–1pm from October to April. As in the UK, many transactions can also be done at *cajas de ahorros* (savings banks) which sometimes keep longer hours. Money can be changed (*cambio*) at hotels, and bureaux de change travel agents.

Post Offices (*Oficinas de Correos*) open at least 9am–1pm Monday to Saturday, with main ones open all day. Stamps (*sellos*) can be bought in tobacconists (called *estancos*, but look for a brown and yellow 'T' sign saying '*tabacos*'). They can also be bought at most hotel receptions.

Main Post Offices (for Poste Restante (*Lista de Correos*) mail):
Seville: Avenida de la Constitución 32. Tel: 95 421 95 85.
Córdoba: Calle Cruz Conde 21. Tel: 957 47 91 96.
Granada: Puerta Real 1. Tel: 958 22 11 38.

HEALTH & EMERGENCIES

Beware the sun's beguiling strength. It is very easy to get burnt, even up in the cooler mountains. Use a strong suntan cream and always drink bottled water.

For minor health problems chemists (*farmacias*) are a good source of advice. They are devoted solely to dispensing medication and are marked by a green cross. Don't confuse them with *droguerías* which sell perfume and toiletries. *Farmacias* have a rota of after-hours service (*farmacia de guardia*) – to find this look for a sign posted in the window or in the local paper. For a doctor (*médico*) or dentist (*dentista*) ask at a hotel or in the Tourist Office.

State facilities are adequate – form E111, available from the main post offices in the UK, entitles British citizens to certain benefits in Spain, but if you want to take advantage of these you must first get treatment vouchers from the Instituto Nacional de la Seguridad Social (INSS), and then you can only go to doctors who operate the scheme. Good medical insurance is a better bet.

Emergencies

Police and Emergency (*urgencia*) 091.
Fire Brigade 080.
Medical emergency: 061
Seville 95 442 55 65.
Córdoba 957 29 55 70.
Granada 958 28 20 00.

First Aid station (*Casa de Socorro*):
Seville: Menendez y Pelayo.
Tel: 954 41 17 12.
Córdoba: Avenida Dr Blanco Soler,
4 Tel 957 21 77 78.
Granada: Avenida de la Constitución
(Main Hospital). Tel: 958 24 11 00.

Police

Policemen come in three different colours. In urban areas the *Policía Nacional* (dark blue uniforms) rule the streets while the *Policía Municipal* (blue uniforms with a white band on their caps) control the traffic. The *Guardia Civil* (olive-green uniforms) rule everything else. Despite the sunglasses and swaggers they're all quite helpful.

Should anything happen tell your hotel or holiday representative, who should then help you inform the Policía Nacional and make a statement for insurance purposes.

Guardian of the streets

If you are travelling independently enlist the help of a resident to interpret. Main police stations are:
Seville: Plaza de la Gavidia.
Tel: 95 422 88 40.
Córdoba: Avenida del Dr Fleming 2.
Tel: 957 47 75 00.
Granada: Plaza de los Campos.
Tel: 958 28 21 50.

Toilets

Pop into a bar, hotel or restaurant and use the *servicios* (sometimes *aseos*) – it is polite to ask permission first.

Insight Guide: Southern Spain (Apa Publications) offers up-to-date information and in-depth essays on Andalusia and the Costa del Sol.
Insight Pocket Guide: Costa del Sol (Apa Publications). Tailor-made itineraries linking the best of the coast and its hinterland.

Poems of Arab Andalusia translated by Cola Franzen (City Lights Books) will transport you straight back to the world of al-Andalus. Miguel de Cervantes's *Exemplary Novels* are cautionary tales from 17th-century Spain and a good warm-up prior to tackling *Don Quixote* (both Penguin Classics). Washington Irving's *Tales of the Alhambra* is essential Granada reading (you can buy it in Granada as a paperback). *Here in Spain* (Lookout) by David Mitchell is a compendium of quotes from travellers in Spain, including quips from Richard Ford's definitive 1845 guide *A Handbook for Travellers in Spain* (Centaur, 3 volumes) and George Borrow's eccentric bible-hawking autobiography *The Bible in Spain* (Century).

From this century Gerald Brenan's *South from Granada* (Cambridge) describes his life in the Alpujarras in the 1920s; Ian Gibson's *Federico García Lorca* (Faber) is a biography of Spain's greatest modern poet. Alistair Boyd's *The Road to Ronda* (Collins) and Penelope Chetwode's *Two Middle-Aged Ladies in Andalusia* (Century) describe horse-riding trips in the 1960s. Nicholas Luard's *Andalucía* (Century) and Hugh Seymour-Davies' *The Bottlebrush Tree* (Constable) tell of life in an Andalusian village.

In the UK, books on Spain can be ordered through world-travel book specialist Daunt Books, 83 Marylebone High St, London W1M 3DE, tel: 020-7224 2295.

Ibn-al-Ahmar 12, 55
Inquisition 12, 13
Irving, Washington 14, 55, 59, 88
Itálica 10, 17, 22, 34, 35, 79

ART & PHOTO CREDITS

Photography
2/3 Stuart Abraham
40, 41 J. D. Dallet
10T, 11, 12B, 13, 14, Nigel Tisdall
25, 29B, 30, 31, 33B,
34T, 35, 45, 47, 51,
53, 54, 56, 60, 61,
63B, 64, 65, 68T, 70,
71, 72, 73T, 74, 76,
78, 79, 80, 84T, 85, 87
1, 12T, 16, 23, 26, 28, Lyle Lawson
43, 46, 48, 50, 58T, 59,
68B, 69, 75, 82, 84B
62, 63T Capilla Real
8/9, 15, 37B, 38B Andrew Eames
10B, 21, 24T, 29T, 58B, Junta de Andalucia
66T, 73B, 77, 81, 88
32, 33T St John O'Rourke
8, 24, 34B, 66B, 67 Alice Prier
36, 37T, 38T, 39, 41, 42, 43 Don Murray

Cover Design Klaus Geisler
Cartography Berndtson & Berndtson

NOTES

The World o

400 books in three complementary serie

nsight Guides

ver every major destination in every continent.

Bhutan★
Boston★
British Columbia★
Brittany★
Brussels★
Budapest & Surroundings★
Canton★
Chiang Mai★
Chicago★
Corsica★
Costa Blanca★
Costa Brava★
Costa del Sol/Marbella★
Costa Rica★
Crete★
Denmark★
Fiji★
Florence★
Florida★
Florida Keys★
French Riviera★
Gran Canaria★
Hawaii★
Hong Kong★
Hungary
Ibiza★
Ireland★
Ireland's Southwest★
Israel★
Istanbul★
Jakarta★
Jamaica★
Kathmandu Bikes & Hikes★
Kenya★
Kuala Lumpur★
Lisbon★
Loire Valley★
London★
Macau
Madrid★
Malacca
Maldives
Mallorca★
Malta★
Mexico City★
Miami★
Milan★
Montreal★
Morocco★
Moscow
Munich★

Nepal★
New Delhi
New Orleans★
New York City★
New Zealand★
Northern California★
Oslo/Bergen★
Paris★
Penang★
Phuket★
Prague★
Provence★
Puerto Rico★
Quebec★
Rhodes★
Rome★
Sabah★
St Petersburg★
San Francisco★
Sardinia
Scotland★
Seville★
Seychelles★
Sicily★
Sikkim
Singapore★
Southeast England
Southern California★
Southern Spain★
Sri Lanka★
Sydney★
Tenerife★
Thailand★
Tibet★
Toronto★
Tunisia★
Turkish Coast★
Tuscany★
Venice★
Vienna★
Vietnam★
Yogyakarta
Yucatan Peninsula★

★ = *Insight Pocket Guides with Pull out Maps*

Insight Compact Guides

Algarve
Amsterdam
Bahamas
Bali
Bangkok

Barbados
Barcelona
Beijing
Belgium
Berlin
Brittany
Brussels
Budapest
Burgundy
Copenhagen
Costa Brava
Costa Rica
Crete
Cyprus
Czech Republic
Denmark
Dominican Republic
Dublin
Egypt
Finland
Florence
Gran Canaria
Greece
Holland
Hong Kong
Ireland
Israel
Italian Lakes
Italian Riviera
Jamaica
Jerusalem
Lisbon
Madeira
Mallorca
Malta
Milan
Moscow
Munich
Normandy
Norway
Paris
Poland
Portugal
Prague
Provence
Rhodes
Rome
St Petersburg
Salzburg
Singapore
Switzerland
Sydney
Tenerife
Thailand

Turkey
Turkish Coast
Tuscany
UK regional titles:
Bath & Surroundings
Cambridge & East Anglia
Cornwall
Cotswolds
Devon & Exmoor
Edinburgh
Lake District
London
New Forest
North York Moors
Northumbria
Oxford
Peak District
Scotland
Scottish Highlands
Shakespeare Country
Snowdonia
South Downs
York
Yorkshire Dales
USA regional titles:
Boston
Cape Cod
Chicago
Florida
Florida Keys
Hawaii: Maui
Hawaii: Oahu
Las Vegas
Los Angeles
Martha's Vineyard & Nantucket
New York
San Francisco
Washington D.C.
Venice
Vienna
West of Ireland